DENTAL PRACTICE
STRATEGY GUIDE

Practical Advice to Help You Evaluate Your Business Options
Through All Phases of Your Dental Career

DR. RANDALL M. LAFROM

FOREWORD BY SCOTT J. MANNING, MBA

DENTAL BUSINESS STRATEGY SERIES

FOREWORD

Once in a career on a journey of a lifetime you might be so lucky as to meet someone who will change your perspective, challenge your thinking, open your mind to the possibilities, and guide you into something greater, with more certainty and confidence, and less guesswork and trial and errors.

This person would be one revered and sought out from far and nearby peers who wish to climb to the top of the mountain that he has, where he remains, at the pinnacle of his chosen profession—that just so happens to be yours too.

Introducing Dr. Randall LaFrom.

I meet lots of dentists, thousands still today. I've talked to as many Doctors personally, gotten inside of their heads, and gotten a feel for their practices as much as anyone else alive. Over all this time, I've met interesting people. I say 'people' not just 'Doctors' because we are after all, 'people', first and foremost.

One person stands out in my mind as the most well-rounded success story as regards balance of life, clinical achievements, practice success and overall great guy - Dr. Randall LaFrom.

It has been my truest pleasure to get to know Dr. LaFrom and watch him on his journey from Master Clinician and successful practice owner to a thought leader in the industry and a 'been there done that,' *tried and true in the trenches guide* for others Doctors.

You can't mistake his passion – it motivates him. You can't keep up with his energy – it drives him. You can't fathom his desire to help you succeed – until you meet him. Most people are big talkers. Dr. LaFrom is a doer, he always has been.

Be certain that in these pages is a great opportunity to find that shortcut to your success, to benefit from his expedition through dentistry. You'll find the reassurance that only comes from shared stories, hopes, dreams, and the challenges of someone who has empathy because they have been there, who has wisdom because they have fought the good fight, and won.

You are holding in your hands; something very special. Life altering, practice changing, team transforming, something like a compass into your future – for your career; a map, a crystal ball, something so powerful that you can't possibly grasp its worth until you've experienced it, one page, one stage, one chapter at a time.

When you turn to others for knowledge and direction it's wise to seek out advice from someone who has seen it all, who has undeniable passion and experience, and above all else; who wants to provide you with what is best for you - not someone who just wants to sell you a bill of goods of changing trends, or someone who wants to sway you down some path because it matches their agenda.

Know this, you can never experience or learn enough in one lifetime to solve all the problems you'll encounter and overcome all the challenges that will come your way—you must leverage the knowledge and experience of others.

There is no other Dentist, Entrepreneur, Businessperson, Intellectual, or *'been through it all* Doctor' I know that brings together the disciplined organization that most doctors lack, and the need and the creative vision of possibilities that all doctors wish they had, and often think they do.

Inside of this book, you are about to go on a journey, and you are well-placed in the hands of the best guide I know to take you on this path—caring, understanding, authentic, and yet tough—focused on helping you get all you can out of the profession you have chosen.

Isn't it time to arm yourself with the information necessary to help YOU? After all you've spent your education and time focusing on everyone else.

Dr. Randall LaFrom is the Dentist's Doctor. His mind is expansive, his vision limitless, his knowledge intense, and above all else; his desire to help YOU so immense that; just holding this book in your hands; you're already better off.

Do yourself the biggest favor you can, you've read a lot of textbooks, you've experienced a lot of things, none more important than the real-life experiment you wake up to every single day: Your career, business, practice, profession – Dentistry.

Devour this book, study it's content, choose your own adventure, and latch on to Dr. LaFrom, and don't let go, because I can tell you this: I've never met someone with the intuitive ability to help another dentist through their career like this dentist right here.

Your trust is well placed. Your time well invested. Now it's up to you to make the most of it. I can promise you, Dr. LaFrom will make certain that's exactly what happens.

Scott J Manning MBA.

Author of The Dental Practice Shift and 6 other Provocative Dental Business Books. Industry Renegade and Practice Revolutionary.

www.DentalSuccessToday.com

THE DENTAL PRACTICE
STRATEGY GUIDEBOOK

TABLE OF CONTENTS

Introduction		**7**
SECTION ONE – Stages In Your Dental Career		**13**
Chapter One	The New Graduate	13
Chapter Two	The Experienced Dentist	17
Chapter Three	The Advanced Dentist	37
SECTION TWO – Creating The Structure For Success		**43**
Chapter Four	The Successful Organization	43
SECTION THREE – Dental Practice Business Models		**57**
Chapter Five	Solo Practice	57
Chapter Six	Associateships	69
Chapter Seven	Partnerships	81
Chapter Eight	Space Sharing	83
Chapter Nine	Bringing in a Specialist	89
Chapter Ten	Solo-Group Practice	91
Chapter Eleven	Corporate Dentistry	93
SECTION FOUR – Retirement Transition Strategies		**99**
Chapter Twelve	Build Your Practice - Then have Associate(s) run it	99
Chapter Thirteen	Selling Your Practice – Continue to Work as an Associate	101
Chapter Fourteen	Selling Your Practice - Retire	105
SECTION FIVE – What's Next?		**125**
Chapter Fifteen	Enjoying your Retirement Lifestyle the Way You Deserve To	132
References and Resources		**134**
Appendix		**135**

INTRODUCTION

The **DENTAL PRACTICE STRATEGY GUIDEBOOK** was written as a lifetime reference book for Dentists. Once you receive your degree from Dental School, your options are limitless. It is like having a license to learn and master the business side of Dentistry while refining and expanding your clinical skills. Not only is the actual implementation and delivery of dentistry constantly changing, but the options of what environment or structure in which you deliver is also evolving.

This is YOUR LIFE. Each day you will be faced with new decisions either from a clinical standpoint or from a business perspective. Those people who make the best decisions will most likely be the most successful in this career. Everyone has a different set of personal circumstances as well as personality traits that guide their own thoughts and ideas. Asking colleagues what they think you should or should not do can be helpful, but it would be nice to have a trusted mentor to help guide you through some of the tougher decisions. New governmental regulations, new technologies, the Internet, new ways of marketing, dealing with third-party payers, deciding whether to go solo or join a group, when you should incorporate—or if you should incorporate—these are all topics *not* covered in great detail at dental school. The clinical procedures and business strategies that worked in dental practices 20 - 30 years ago would be outdated and minimally useful today.

The role of technology in every field is evolving and improving the delivery of services and the processing of information. As with most professions today, dentists need to be willing to embrace technology and can't be complacent about their level of knowledge when it comes to using computers. Most younger people are taught to use computers in school, but 25 years ago, this was not the case. Many older dentists admit to barely being able to turn on a computer much less fully utilizing the vast array of software and products that are available today. *Dentists MUST embrace technology* in order to stay current. If not, they are leaving themselves at the mercy of their younger staff, or may not be able to monitor their business properly and watch out for embezzlement or lack of proper and accurate documentation.

Running a dental practice means running a business. It means dealing with third-party payers, insurance companies, corporate competition, and implementing proper bookkeeping and accounting systems. It means training and motivating a team, and dealing with all the new governmental regulations and business guidelines that all influence what YOUR next step should be. Every few years, a dentist needs to re-evaluate where they are currently in their practice and where they would like to be going in the future. For example, are you looking to integrate new technology, add an associate, become an associate, expand your facilities, specialize in one aspect of dentistry, join a group practice, or transition out of dentistry in the next 3-5 years? If so, this guidebook is designed to give you some insights and help prepare you for those types of transitions in your career.

A key thing to remember is that this profession is going to be encompassing a significant portion of your daily life. *Dentistry is a people business.* While being financially successful is good, if the daily routine of the business is not fulfilling, then it can become an **empty** success. They say that if you love helping others and you love what you are doing, then you'll never "work" a day in your life. Building a successful dental practice takes work...hard work, and persistence. Many dentists mention that once they get to that **next level** in their practice, THEN they will feel successful. It's almost like pursuing that carrot on the end of a stick. The target keeps moving. We must learn to enjoy the journey, as that is where we will be spending the majority of our time.

Dentistry is a relationship business. Your **core values**, which are your internal beliefs about how life should be, may help guide you in your choices of which path to take in your career. Examples of some core values are integrity, respect, teamwork, quality, collaboration, advancing research, fun, cost-consciousness, leadership, innovation, delivering a WOW experience, compassion, and creating value. Different dental practice styles may embrace or focus on certain core values more than others. Some people believe that when the primary focus of a business is profitability that it may violate some other core values of that business. The policies and practices of a business must, in fact, live up to the core values of the business entity. *Success* can be defined as more than just the productivity of the organization but also the ability to live up to the core values of the group.

In addition to core values, *Dentistry is about building a **CULTURE**. This is how you interact* with others on your journey of a shared goal. It is about the communication you have with each member on your team as well as with your clients. It's about the energy and feel of the business.

*Dentistry is about pushing past the **barriers** to success.* Some of these barriers will be financial - such as student loans, business equipment loans, etc., or prioritization. Some might be personal - such as leadership, discipline, health, family, or age. Others might be external forces - such as competition, 3rd party insurance plan influence, technology, available staffing, or shifts in the marketplace. There are also invisible barriers that are perceived and are not tangible. Such barriers could include a lack of confidence, experience, or the ability to confront challenges and setbacks. These situations often are tackled best with an experienced colleague or *clinical coach* or a *business coach* who advises and helps you see beyond your own personal experience into what is actually possible. A competent business coach or mentor can help you apply fundamental laws of business and management strategies to transform situations and influence others as you turn your vision into a reality.

The purpose of this book is to help you consider things you didn't think of, ask the right questions, reflect on your own core values and personal circumstances, and then help you focus on pursuing the best options throughout your career. You are currently holding in your hands; one of the most up-to-date books available, covering the broad range of topics to help you avoid the pitfalls and make better decisions in your career.

There was an excellent article written for the American Dental Association titled "**Critical Trends Affecting the Future of Dentistry; Assessing the Landscape**". It was published in March 2013 by Diringer and Associates, and in it, they identified several emerging trends affecting the future of dental healthcare in the United States.

Some of these trends included the following:

- An increased competition for dental patients and an increased push for alternative practice models for cost-effectiveness. This is especially true for the younger population who have their care delivered through Preferred Provider Programs or Managed Care Programs.

- The increasing aged population that prefers more personal interactions with the dentist as well as owning lesser dental insurance coverage (allowing for lesser restrictions on choice of dentist).

- The increasing debt on new graduating dentists (averaging over $262,000) affecting their decisions to either delay or forego the solo practice model until much later. In fact, nearly three times as many dentists who graduated in the last ten years have gone into group practices and corporate models as opposed to those who graduated in the prior ten-year period.

- The demographics of the new dentists – with 60 percent of the younger dentists under the age of 44 being women. Nearly 50% of them prefer to work part-time and either be associates or employees.

- We have more educated consumers who are better informed decision makers.

In addition, there has been a measurable increase in public dental health programs such as Medicaid (for Seniors), Children's Health Insurance Program (CHIP), Coordinated Care Organizations, and Community Health Centers that are providing care for the underserved populations, including the elderly and lower-income populations. Unfortunately, these programs tend to focus on providing emergency dental care with little attention given to regular maintenance.

Dentists who study these critical trends and implement the necessary modifications in their strategies will thrive in the years ahead. This book will help you to make wiser choices by adding to your base of knowledge with fundamental data and solid business strategies.

SECTION ONE

STAGES IN YOUR DENTAL CAREER

CHAPTER ONE - THE NEW GRADUATE

CHAPTER TWO - THE EXPERIENCED DENTIST

CHAPTER THREE - THE ADVANCED DENTIST

SECTION ONE

STAGES IN YOUR DENTAL CAREER

CHAPTER ONE

THE DENTAL STUDENT GRADUATE OR NEW DENTIST

From the day that you graduated from Dental School you began your transition. You had options and many choices. You could have gone into teaching, started a practice, joined a practice as an associate, continued with specialty training, or undergone a General Practice Residency (GPR). All of a sudden, no one was telling you what you had to do and you had no deadlines. Possibly, the only thing on your mind was how you were going to start paying off your dental school loans.

According to the *American Dental Education Association Survey* conducted in 2016, just over 50% of the graduating dental students planned on going directly into a private practice of some sort (2248 of the approximately 4500 new graduates). One third planned on doing either a **General Practice Residency** (GPR) or going into either a specialty or Dental Internship. A GPR is an intensive post-graduate accredited training program that is designed to enhance the resident's experience, confidence, and broaden their knowledge, typically done in an academic or hospital setting. While the majority of the time is spent in clinic, additional classroom work and lectures go deeper; often into areas such as sedation, implantology, endodontics, surgery, or prosthodontics. In some states, a GPR is a requirement to fully complete the dental training program.

Many new graduates coming out of dental school carry with them school loans averaging upwards of $260,000, according to the A.D.A. survey conducted in 2016. There is high motivation to begin earning money sooner to pay off that debt. This type of financial pressure can impact the reasons that a student went to dental school in the first place. Most students go to dental school because they want to help others, they like the idea of being self-employed and *being their own boss*, they like to control their work schedule, and they enjoy working with their hands in a career that offers creative and artistic outlets. This book can help to *preserve that dream*. One idea alone from this book could affect your decision process and easily help you make or save hundreds of thousands of dollars throughout your lifetime.

Nearly 50% of all graduating students will delay practicing dentistry immediately and consider either a residency or advanced education in a specialty after graduation. Obviously, this is a big decision as it will most likely either add to their debt or minimally chip away at it via an educational residency. If you choose to go GPR, it means taking a lower salary rather than jumping into an associateship right out of school, with the intention of learning more skills in the specialties of dentistry and building up both your diagnostic and treatment planning confidence as well as clinical speed in a "safe" environment under the guidance of more experienced faculty dentists. It also means a longer-term commitment to education along with delay of certain other possibilities such as travel and pursuit of hobbies.

You are like a clean slate. You can create your journey as a dentist and pursue any number of options. If you were fortunate enough to have a parent in practice who has an opportunity open for you, sometimes, that may be the easiest route to getting a job in the dental field.

Perhaps the idea of going into education or research might intrigue you. Dental Schools need teachers periodically, and Dental Researchers and Developers are always looking to create equipment or techniques that make Dentistry easier, more precise, and faster, and in producing materials that are more durable, biocompatible, or more aesthetic.

As mentioned earlier, another option is to specialize in any of the nine recognized post-graduate programs such as Orthodontics and Dentofacial Orthopedics, Periodontics, Oral and Maxillofacial Radiology, Oral and Maxillofacial Surgery, Pediatric Dentistry, Prosthodontics, Public Health, Oral and Maxillofacial Pathology, and Endodontics. These specialties are open to both new graduates as well as dentists who have been in practice for a while who may wish to further their knowledge in a particular area.

Lastly, the option to go directly into private practice is available to you. This could be with another dentist as an associate or a partner, or you may wish to proceed alone. This is often the most commonly desired paths for the majority of new dentists. They went to school to provide dentistry and "be their own boss" so they are eager to go out and practice what they have learned in school.

PRIVATE PRACTICE - ASSOCIATE OR OWNERSHIP?

If you chose to go into private practice, you can start your own practice, join an ongoing practice, or take over the practice of a dentist who is retiring. You could buy a practice or you could associate for several years. There are often financial advantages to owning a business. You are able to write-off more business-related expenses than you could as an associate. Typically, in a well-structured arrangement, as an owner of a dental practice, you should earn more money than an associate dentist would, since they have "skin in the game"—meaning a financial commitment to all the purchases of equipment and loans against the practice. As an owner, you should be earning something from the business as it is your personal funds that are being tied up in equipment or leasehold improvements. The business itself should be earning you at least what it would earn if the same amount of money were sitting in the bank. If not, then you should have a rethink. There is long-term equity being built up when you own your own practice versus being an associate, and that equity also has future value.

If you do work for another dentist after you get out of school, then the question of whether to buy a practice or stay as an associate comes up. If you enjoy the flexibility of not having to deal with all the legal and regulatory issues, or hiring and training employees, then associating can be a good option. (It seems that each year, a new regulation is brought upon the dental industry. If the regulation isn't about concerns over amalgam, it's water-supply lines. Otherwise it's H.I.P.A.A. compliance, and most recently, it's having proper signage, such as gender neutral plaques—on your bathroom door!) If you don't like dealing with all of the changing regulations, ownership may not be the route to take! On the other hand, the statistics show that it works out best financially in the long run to own your business. Below are some statistics to back up that claim. In a subsequent chapter, we will have a deeper discussion on the various practice business models, as well as the options of buying an existing practice versus starting one from scratch.

Dental practices have a less than 1% failure rate. You have the potential to earn an additional 20 - 40% or more income on average as an owner of a practice than as an associate dentist. Some reasons for this include: The ability to write off more expenses, control your overhead as tightly or loosely as you wish, and the fact that you are building equity in your own business, which you could sell as an asset when you are ready to retire. If you purchase your building and it appreciates along with your practice over the years, it adds another bonus to being an owner. These numbers can add up to millions over your lifespan as a dentist. Of course, there is the trade-off of using your capital (or more loans) to achieve that position.

If you purchase an ongoing dental practice versus starting up one from the ground up, you should be able to see an immediate income stream. When you start from scratch, typically it will take six months before you can see any true income. For this reason, it would be prudent to have *six months anticipated overhead* covered in your bank account (referred to as *working capital*) on top of any equipment and facilities loan on a new practice.

CONSIDERATIONS RELATED TO PERSONAL, EMOTIONAL, AND FINANCIAL DECISIONS

If you are single vs. married and trying to raise a family of several children, the incentive might be to get out and start making money as soon as you can. Your ability to manage your finances, hire and train employees, negotiate leases, and sell dentistry would determine your "readiness" to step out on your own.

It probably takes on average between 2 - 3 years before most dentists feel ready or comfortable, from a business and clinical perspective; to start their own business. For the first few years out of school you are still improving your skills, your speed, and your ability to communicate needed treatment to patients. If you don't have that down and you add on the pressures and financial stress of running a business, it could become a potential recipe for disaster. Dental school tends to offer very little training in the way of team-building, goal-setting, staff-training and hiring, much less finding out that patients may not accept or believe everything that you tell them. Many dental schools do realize this and this is why they often encourage (or even require) a general practice residency (GPR) option for their students to gain more clinical expertise and speed to help counterbalance the lack of business training.

It may seem hard to believe that just 40+ years ago, most dentists would simply go out and start a business right as they got out of school and by implementing good decisions, could do well. As they got older, many dentists would just slow down, close up their shop and walk away when they retired. These days, the options for using your practice as an integral part of your overall retirement strategy is becoming more and more necessary. This is discussed in greater detail later in the book.

SECTION ONE

STAGES IN YOUR DENTAL CAREER

CHAPTER TWO

THE EXPERIENCED DENTIST

The EXPERIENCED Dentist is one that is growing their practice, working ON their practice systems, and expanding their services, while developing their leadership skills. According to the ADA, a general dentist will hit their stride after about 15 - 20 years in practice. They would have acquired the business, leadership, marketing, and clinical skills needed to move their practices forward. They would have made mistakes, seen others make mistakes, and taken enough courses; that they hopefully would have become wiser in their decision making. They have developed networks of colleagues and support teams that can help advise them along the way.

According to several financial institutions we interviewed, an established dentist (generally one with over 10 - 15 years' experience) will be able to get close to 100% financing on most dental equipment or expansion projects they are interested in pursuing. They could typically receive twice the amount a new graduate could. Why? Of course, it's obvious. They have a proven track record of running a business or generating income.

At this stage in your career, assuming you are in private practice in some form or another, the thoughts of adapting your business strategies to change things up often come about. These could include: expanding of your facilities, remodeling your office, moving into a nicer office, taking some new courses to expand your clinical skills, purchasing a new large piece of equipment to aid in providing patient care, hiring an associate, joining with another dentist and/or forming a partnership. These are all viable options and they each come with opportunities and consequences.

At this point in your career, it's time to start (if you haven't already) spending some time with a financial planner to plot out your next steps. Planning for things such as college education for children, weddings, helping with down payments for your children's first home, charities, life insurance, buying or selling a home, divorces, marriages and more, all can impact how solid your decisions as to what to do next are. Making sure that you are funding your own retirement plan is always a good idea, since you are self-employed, no one will be doing it for you.

This is a good period to look at your time and the financial resources that you use for growing your practice to make sure that they are in balance with your family and professional objectives. This is the best way to create sustainable growth.

Below are listed, many commonly used strategies for Growing/Improving an established Dental Practice, (they are elaborated on in the section that follows):

A. Hiring a Business Coach or a Mentor.

B. Remodeling, Painting, Office Expansions.

C. Hiring a Dental Hygienist.

D. Moving to a New Location.

E. Refining Your Skills as a Leader.

F. Refining Your Skills as a Marketer.

G. Refining Your Skills as a Communicator.

H. Building up Your Practice, Bring in an Associate or Specialist.

I. Adding a Second (or Third) Location.

J. Buying Another Practice.

K. Creating Solid Business Systems.

L. Purchasing Your Own Building to Practice In.

M. Signing Up for a Preferred Provider Dental Benefits Plan.

N. Investing in Additional Clinical Training or Advanced Equipment.

O. Restructuring your Loans.

P. Being Different.

Q. Establishing some Type of Retirement Plan.

R. Purging Your Stuff.

S. Getting involved in your Local Community.

A.   HIRING A BUSINESS COACH OR MENTOR:

One of the best investments you can make is in **yourself**. If you hire a coach, you can use their knowledge to push past your own barriers and identify those that you didn't even know were in your way. It can make going through practice transitions easier when you have someone who has done it, and or knows what to look for and how to make it happen smoothly. A good business coach will help guide you into the future with a more solid team, sound business systems and stronger leadership skills. A business coach can help you push yourself out of your comfort zone and help you and your team get to the next level and grow your business.

B.   REMODELING, PAINTING, OFFICE EXPANSIONS:

If you decide to remodel your office or simply re-carpet or repaint it, these actions, for some reason, increases the practice income almost immediately. It excites the staff, impresses to the patients that you are stepping up your game, improves staff morale, and frequently brings a positive energy to the office. It shows others that you are investing in your environment and reinvesting in your business, rather than putting the deposit down on your next sports car or vacation.

If you are choosing to expand your office facilities, first make sure that you are utilizing the current facilities to the maximum. Is there a room that doesn't get used that could be converted to consolidate two functions or free up space (such as a staff room/consult room/larger supply storage area)? Can one of the rooms have a dual purpose? When you expand your facility, you expand your monthly rent expense as well, increasing your overhead. So, the key is to make sure that you can expand in a manner that will pay for itself. For example, if your hygiene department needs more space, and it would allow you to add another couple more days of hygiene to expand, then it would make financial sense to do that. If there is need for a storage space for charts, perhaps there is a basement, or storage space down the street that might be cheaper to put your old models or charts or excess supplies in, rather than adding to your facility overhead.

Expanding your facility should not be taken lightly. If patients are having to wait a couple of months for treatment because you simply don't have the space to see them, but you have the energy and capability to see them, then the added space will be beneficial. Sometimes it is useful to consider more effective scheduling of patients to maximize rooms and hit daily practice goals. This is most beneficial when you are limited to two or possibly three chairs to work out of. You may have a certain number of patients that are having bleaching trays delivered, nightguard impressions, ortho wires put on or replaced, etc. and this could be done in a spare operatory. Make sure you determine if it needs to be fully outfitted or if it can be used more for exams and simpler procedures. If so, that could potentially save you over $20,000 worth of unnecessary expense for setting up a fully functional additional treatment room. Always think long term and *what's next?* If you may eventually have an associate working out of the room, then make sure it is not too cramped, understocked, or under-equipped. Adding a treatment room can potentially add another 15 - 35% productivity to an office if done correctly and at the right time.

There is a second aspect of the actual cost of expanding a building. In addition to what you pay the contractor, you need to consider the potential disruption to the practice during construction. If it's a small project, then let it be accomplished in the evening and wrapped up over the weekend, (this is always better from the standpoint of potential patient treatment "downtime"). If there will be lots of drilling and hammering and dust, then you may need to shut down the business for a few days or more as construction continues, with walls being taken down or carpeting being laid. When you add in the potential disruption to your treatment schedule, that could end up costing a significant amount. Depending upon the extent of the change, you might even need to utilize a separate facility, such as a neighbor's office, as an interim operations place. If you are knocking out walls, plan on getting permits and coordinating the various contractors and cabinetry people since they often need to have one stage of the project completed before the next one begins. One minor set-back can trigger an expensive delay.

Be careful if you are doing a significant amount of expansion on an old building. Sometimes, it may require that you expand a bathroom to make it wheelchair-accessible (if it's not) and that could mean adding several extra thousand dollars to the cost to expand the facility. If you bring in a competent architect or space planner, they may be able to help with suggestions on how to minimize your overall costs while achieving a desired goal.

Expanding your hours of operation is typically an easy way to produce more. By adding more convenient *earlier-in-the-day* or *later-in-the-evening* appointments, or Saturdays, you will attract many people who work 8am - 5pm. The only problem is, if you build your practice based upon this, and in a few years decide not to continue those hours, you will potentially lose many of those patients that changed over due to the more convenient timing.

B. HIRING A DENTAL HYGIENIST:

One of the common stages in dental practice growth is hiring a dental hygienist for your practice. If you started out doing all the dental cleanings yourself in a practice, sometimes it can be difficult to give up that part of the relationship and bonding time with your patients. In addition, the hygienist is an extension of your personality and your care. It is important that you communicate regularly about clinical care and preventive care concepts. You want to make sure you are both on the same page when patients ask questions about topics like electric toothbrushes, fluoride, flossing, mouth rinses, supplemental periodontal medicaments, teeth-whitening options, what toothpastes to use, lasers, nutritional counseling, etc. It is important to remember that not only can a hygienist potentially add to the practice income directly, but by taking the hygiene appointments out of your schedule, you are allowed the opportunity to spend that time taking on more profitable and clinically challenging procedures. Finally, the hygienist can be a helpful partner in pre-diagnosing treatment or identifying conditions that are less than ideal in a patient's mouth. They can prepare the patient in advance so that they can show the doctor areas that they might be concerned about as well.

D. MOVING TO A NEW LOCATION:

Obviously, moving to a new location requires more thought than simply expanding a practice location. Unless your building is being torn down and you unavoidably have to move, moving to a new location requires months or even years of planning and preparation to make sure that everything goes smoothly. In general, anticipate that it will cost more and take longer than initially planned. Be careful and have a back-up plan. You don't want to have to be scrambling to find a temporary facility to work out of in the event of your plans getting delayed a month or more. You might end up working for a few months in the evenings—Fridays and Saturdays, while your office is being completed. If there is a delay due to weather, scheduling delays, or a contractor not following through on specific items in a timely manner, it can throw off the schedule regarding all the ensuing bits and pieces, including cabinets, carpets, electrical and equipment delivery, etc.

One potentially easier way to move your practice is to purchase an existing practice with a larger beautiful facility in a desirable location. When you merge your practice into an existing practice, you will be able to combine the best systems from both, and possibly the best equipment and staff from both.

E.   REFINING YOUR SKILLS AS A LEADER:

In addition to clinical training, when a dentist takes courses in practice management and personal development, a dentist will grow their practice based upon their ability to effectively market their practice, lead their team, and communicate. Success often comes from creating the environment or the structure for the success to occur in. If your systems are not consistently implemented and the staff are not trained or being held accountable, your growth potential will be limited. Some of the systems that need to be designed and implemented are protocols for: **Hiring and Training Staff**, **Marketing Strategies**, **Creating the New Patient Experience**, and having solid **Financial Systems** in place.

An owner-dentist must also know and implement Human Resource Laws, Dental Practice Laws, follow OSHA and HIPAA guidelines, follow appropriate tax laws all along with providing quality dental care to their patients. Having these systems in place will help SUSTAIN growth because you become pro-active instead of reactive.

LEADERSHIP

As your team begins to grow, the more and more they look to you as their "leader". Most dentist owners are managing, thinking that they are leading. In fact, most dentists become "micro-managers" which can be even worse, and can sabotage your practice or limit your growth. Your team will look at your habits, methods of communication, behavior and your own level of accountability for things that are happening in the practice. It is said that you can "feel the energy" of a practice that is run well, just as you can feel it when people (staff or patients) don't really want to be at the office. These types of attitudes come from management and from the owner of the practice. If you strive to provide excellent comprehensive care and are a leader your team respects, it will show up subtly when your staff present dental care to your clients. This is what creates the "culture" of a practice.

Your ability to inspire people to follow you and put the "team's needs" above their own "personal needs" will separate an amazing business from an average business. When the team works maximally efficiently under your direction, your business can maximize the potential for increased productivity and profitability. When the staff see YOUR commitment to your own success *as well as theirs*, they are more motivated to put in a little extra effort to help you with your vision for your business.

It begins by empowering the people who work for you. If you are constantly micro-managing your team and never give them any authority or autonomy to control an area of the business, they will get discouraged and burnout. The only way you can advance is through proper and effective delegation of activities to your staff. This creates a loyalty to the practice since they feel like they are responsible for the growth of the practice.

Being a leader involves developing leaders within your organization. It also means including the team in the practice goals as well as giving and getting feedback from them on how they feel they are doing and what tools or additional training they feel would be helpful. It means encouraging them and redirecting their activities along the way by checking in periodically on their progress. Don't make communication with your team a "walking down the hallway" conversation. Rather, you should schedule regular team as well as individual meetings with your staff during PRODUCTION TIME to show them that you value their time as well as the office time as part of the business. Realize that what THEY consider a big win for themselves may be different from what you consider a big win. Make sure you acknowledge THEIR BIG wins and don't follow them up with comments negating the win by implying, "...but it would have been better if you did this..." Any win in the correct direction should be acknowledged.

Meetings. Who likes them except the Doctor? Probably, the Doctor doesn't even like them. As the leader of the business, you need to make sure that meetings are productive and have a purpose. You should share the responsibility of leading the meeting with key staff. Be prepared in advance and know the desired outcome of every meeting. Simply reading off names and procedures from the schedule of patients in the *morning huddle* does not epitomize an effective meeting. Notify the team of openings in the schedule: Who requires outstanding treatment, who is due for a cleaning, any insurance pre-authorizations, any large outstanding debts on the patients, any personal situations that are relevant in the patient's lives, how close you are to the goal for the day, as well as what the next few days should look like. These are the conversations that will make the difference. You should also acknowledge any successes in the previous day or period since the last meeting, and identify what upcoming challenges you foresee in the near future.

Commitment and integrity go hand in hand. As personal development and goals performance coach Gary Ryan Blair states, "We sabotage our reputation by not keeping our commitments to ourselves and others. Success is the result of making and keeping your commitments to yourself and others. Your ability to honor your promises directly impacts your credibility, reputation, trustworthiness, earning ability and your overall peace of mind." As the leader of your company, it is critical to maintain integrity with your team and your clients.

Culture is the shared attitudes, beliefs and behaviors that determine how a company's employees and management interact and handle business transactions. Culture evolves over time and it develops from embracing the values put forth by the leadership of the company. Things such as rewarding valuable contributions from staff and others, cultivating positive relationships between employees, encouraging autonomy and giving regular feedback are all great ways to build positive culture.

Employee turnover is very expensive and doesn't look good to clients. In a practice with a high employee turnover, the patients may wonder if one day you will still be there (if they are continually seeing new faces). No great businesses were formed without strong teamwork. If you weren't born with the ability to coach others, hire a coach to help you. There is a saying that you will grow to your limit of being able to manage others. Some people have developed strong empowerment skills and love challenges. Those are the rare doctors that aspire to have 20 offices and 300 employees working for them. The average dentist has barely taken more than one or two courses in business in their lifetime and perhaps a few management seminars. This partly explains why most dentists prefer practicing solo or staying in smaller group practices.

More about LEADERSHIP is discussed in Section Two, Chapter Four.

F. REFINING YOUR SKILLS AS A MARKETER:

Everything a business does is a form of marketing. How the phones are answered, the cleanliness of the office, how friendly your staff are, how welcome you make the clients feel, testimonials – are all part of your marketing message. Marketing differs from advertising in the following way: Marketing is a broader description of what goes on in a business. It encompasses customer relationships and support, sales strategies, community involvement, and public relations. You could have as many marketing strategies for External Marketing (to non-patients) as you might have for Internal Marketing (to current clients). Advertising tends to focus more on the process of letting clients and potential clients know more about your specific products or services. There can be multiple different venues for advertising specific products. By knowing your target market better and which demographic you might be more interested in it, you can maximize the return on investment with your advertising dollar. A simple example of this would be to offer teeth whitening to newly engaged couples prior to their wedding. You might hit up social media more for cosmetic or quick fix options– such as "six-month smiles" or offer lower cost treatment options including easy financing.

Expand your business by expanding the range of services you provide. Rather than focusing on treating only cavities and broken fillings. This could include discussing things like nutrition and total health awareness, sleep apnea, diabetes, dental implants and TMJ. Try expanding your services to include treatment that is not affected by dental benefits plans and creating a niche or special service that is not considered a "*commodity*". A commodity is considered something that is a useful basic service or product that can be purchased anywhere (and from anyone), where the cost is a more important factor than quality.

Having a solid ongoing *internal* and *external marketing* program will help provide for continued sustainable growth for the practice that will improve the bottom line of the business.

More on Marketing is discussed in Section Two, Chapter Four.

G.   REFINING YOUR SKILLS AS A COMMUNICATOR:

COMMUNICATIONS

Communications is basically demonstrated through the efficiency of systems and the flow of people and paperwork through the office. A well-run office is often the result of effective communications starting from the owner-dentist and going down through the team members. One of the first signs of a struggling practice is poor internal communications. Internal communications are those conversations between the Doctor and the team as well as between team members. Effective external communications to the patients (and suppliers and vendors) helps to create an environment of trust and to develop relationships with the patients and makes for a smoother running business.

Communication is the ability to relay information, the ability to influence, the ability to delegate and the ability to get things done through others. The effectiveness of it could be the quality of communication, the quantity of communication, the context, or the timing. Some examples of common communication breakdowns include: (1) The front desk staff are not able to convert callers into clients who will schedule appointments; (2) The dentist can't communicate well enough to the patients how they are able to help them achieve optimal health; (3) The dentist can't communicate well enough to have their team work efficiently and spends 20% of their time having to check on other's work to see if it was done. There are times when it might be more cost effective to invest into training and communications courses for you and your team, rather than simply spending more and more money on clinical training, ineffective marketing, or buying a second practice to merge with.

In some cases, creating scripts and *"role-playing"* with the staff can be an effective tool. While this can make sure the message delivered is accurate and complete, some staff may feel uncomfortable with using scripts. If that is the case, they should practice role-playing with the script a few times, then set it aside and attempt to say it in their own words as they do feel comfortable saying it. It will sound more friendly and smoother if done that way. If you role-play in front of a third-party observer, it adds a dimension of "safe stress" that will aid in getting past the communication barriers to success.

The second and more critical part of communication is listening. Many people are distracted or waiting for the opportunity to say what they want to say and not paying attention or even asking what the other person really wants. Effective listening involves listening for "cues" in the conversation – for what is said, as well as what is NOT said. Listen to hear if they understand what you are saying. Check in with the other person throughout your conversation to make sure they are following and in agreement or not. Listen for the other person's concerns and issues. Acknowledge those concerns and then attempt to resolve them or give them the tools or resources to empower them to be able to resolve them. By doing so, you create value.

We all learnt how to talk when we were kids. Talking and effective communication are two different things. You can talk with someone, but if you don't have their full attention or if they don't have the proper framework for what you are saying, appreciate the urgency of what you are saying, or the impact of what you are requesting, there can be communication breakdowns. For instance, "as soon as possible" to one person might mean as soon as they don't have anything else to do, whereas to the person making the request, it might have meant "within minutes". People are not mind-readers. Without specific parameters and timelines, people will use their own timelines and criteria for completion.

One skill that can make or break an office is the dentist's ability to communicate effectively with both their team and their patients in a timely manner, with empathy and compassion, while being confident in what they are offering.

H. BUILDING-UP YOUR PRACTICE, BRINGING IN AN ASSOCIATE OR SPECIALIST

This option seems to have the most potential for long-term money coming in, as you still own the business, and you and your associate are continuing to build equity in the business which you own. Eventually, you can cut back your own hours and enjoy a new lifestyle that allows you to continue practicing but at the same time enjoy your hobbies and travel or do whatever you wish. From a purely economic or financial perspective, many times, hiring an associate may not provide you with a huge additional net income initially, especially for the first few months, when they are learning your systems, you are passing work on to them that you might have done, and they are building the rapport with the patients. Over time, the newer dentist would get more comfortable with presenting treatment and doing comprehensive diagnosis. Sometimes, the newer associate, while taking on more of the traditional dentistry, may afford the owner more time to pursue other things such as specialty niche dentistry, or simply focus on the specific procedures they enjoy more. The trade-off of having an associate is that it often adds to the overhead because of their salary, and not to mention, frequently, additional support staff may be needed to help them as well. More on timing and selection of an associate to work in your practice is covered in Section Three.

If your mental acuity and physical stamina are fitting, bringing in an associate or specialist is a wonderful option for those dentists who enjoy practicing dentistry and simply can't see themselves retiring and doing nothing. If you sell your practice, you no longer have as much control over which patients you see, when you work, or what procedures you can perform. However, there are ways of structuring the transition, such that you can still benefit and enjoy continuing your practice. More discussion on this is handled in Section Four. If you still own your practice, then you will still be the one making the rules as you have done for years, but yet you can give your associate some of the work you chose not to do anymore.

I. ADDING A SECOND (OR THIRD) LOCATION

The skills you had used to build up your first location are *different* from the skills needed to add a second, or for that matter, third or more locations. There are specific personality types that can handle the demands of multiple locations and dealing with building teams and marketing for each location.

This option works well if you are a specialist and you are not completely busy in one practice and you wish to reach into a nearby community or minimize potential competition from other specialists close by. For a general dentist, this may also work, but it often requires a committed associate or partner to pull this off well. Running a dental practice can be expensive, and adding a second practice can double your overhead. When you consider that associates rarely outproduce an owner-dentist, and they typically may not be as committed or invested in the development of a practice, it has the potential to not be as profitable as simply focusing on a single practice. If you have learned how to manage associates well and are willing to work at the second location yourself (even if part-time) it will show your commitment to the practice, and increase your chances for success.

If you have a wildly successful practice and you have people coming in from out of the area, or are working your facility to full capacity, and have patients asking if you would open a second location closer, then you might have some of the makings for a successful second practice.

The challenges are many. One example is, if you have two offices you work out of that are close by each other, you may run the chance of a patient meeting you at the wrong facility from time to time. If both offices are close-by, it may not end up being more that a minor inconvenience for them to rush over to the other facility. If you are at your second location, the patients from the first location will have to travel to your other location if they have a specific issue that needs immediate attention. (Hopefully, you will have access to digital records and having ready access to their charts will not be another issue).

Financially speaking, the costs of this type of task could be successfully minimized by renting space or sharing a facility with another dentist in a different area. That way, the additional overhead would be minimal. This could also work well in a rural area where there may either be a shortage of dentists or a small population to support one dentist in a community. This type of arrangement in general, works better for a specialist, since they tend to draw from a broader area. If they have a satellite office in a new community, they can tap into the population there and serve their needs as well. In addition, since a specialist typically provides a narrower spectrum of services, they wouldn't typically need as large of a stock of supplies at each location. Patients have come to expect to wait or travel to see a specialist, but when it comes to choosing a primary care dentist, convenience (meaning location) is often one of the top reasons for choosing them. The biggest disadvantage a general dentist shoulders trying to build two offices is that it dilutes their energy and increases their marketing dollars.

As elaborated upon later, if you have two locations, the idea of hauling physical charts back and forth can become a burden. As more and more offices go "chartless" and all digital, with x-rays and charting, the process becomes more painless. Being able to access all treatment notes and x-rays from any location can be very convenient.

J.   BUYING ANOTHER PRACTICE

Buying another dental practice has proven to be one of the fastest ways to grow a business. Large corporations have found that buying another business is a great way to increase their market share and reduce competition. The same can potentially be said about buying another practice and merging it with yours (either moving to that location or bringing them to you.) There are several factors that need to be evaluated in advance for this to work well financially:

LOCATION. Will you be keeping the second office open, or merging either your practice into it or the new practice into your facility? By identifying the number of true active patients (typically considered to be those who have been attended to within the past 2 years), you can decide if your current facility has the room and staffing to absorb the new influx of patients. If the other office has a bigger facility, better location, and newer equipment, it might make sense to merge your practice into the other office. The third possibility is to maintain both offices and hire new associates (or even the selling dentist) and split your time at both. This works well if you have successfully found the formula for growth in your initial practice. If you are finding that marketing isn't working, and managing and finding good staffing to be an issue, it might make sense to simply combine the two practices and pick the best equipment and staff from each to create one larger practice.

STAFFING. Will you be keeping the staff (and potentially the selling doctor on as an associate or partner) as part of the arrangement? If both practices are small, most likely you should be picking out the top staff and trying to hold on to them. Most often, when a dentist sells their practice, they are planning on retiring either right then or soon. However, as we will discuss in Section Four, there are some other options available that can be favorable to both the purchasing dentist as well as the selling dentist.

If the facility can support having the selling dentist assist with the transition and stay with the practice for at least 3 - 6 months, this is often a good option. It allows the selling dentist time to round up involved cases, while introducing the new owner, and that can help significantly with the typical attrition observed when a practice is sold. Patients typically might stay because of a prior friendship with the selling dentist, or because they appreciated their unique practice style (which may have even kept people driving a distance to see the old dentist). Patients who have to drive a longer distance because they used to live nearby but moved most likely will transfer to a new dental location closer, since now they require a new dentist treat them anyways.

BUYING CHARTS ONLY. Are you buying the facility, the equipment and the staff, or just the charts? If the selling dentist's office has a lot of older outdated equipment and their lease is up, or they are selling because their poor health is causing the practice to dwindle, buying just the patient database of charts is a very inexpensive way to gain new patients. You already have a section of the population that is used to coming in to see the dentist, they will need to find a new dentist anyways, and if your selling doctor writes a good enough letter to sell you to the patients, you can purchase a set of charts only for about 20% of the value of the potential practice price when it was thriving.

COMPUTERS AND EQUIPMENT. One major concern that wasn't an issue twenty years ago is the merging of two dental practices with duplicate high-tech expensive equipment and unique practice management systems. If you need to convert a large database of patients over to a new system, it can take months to do correctly and/or you can hire data transfer personnel to assist you in completing the process sooner. This would translate to added expense. Should you decide to keep two locations, you can keep your data "in the cloud" so you can access it from anywhere. Training staff on new software, while not impossible, is sometimes a frustrating task and needs to be considered in the expense sheet of the purchase.

SIZE OF THE PATIENT BASE IN RELATION TO THE PRACTICE GROSS. Some dentists have never referred out any procedure (to specialists) and have completed all the dentistry on patients. This type of practice may *not* have as much potential from a financial perspective, compared to one which has a lot of patients and that the dentist hasn't done much dentistry on the patients and mostly repairs and refers out all specialty work. A practice that has 800 - 1000 active patients and grosses $1,200,000 a year (and does it all) might not be as desirable a purchase as one that has 600 - 800 patients and only grosses $400,000 per year (and refers out a lot of dentistry). The reason is that the second practice in addition to letting the dentistry walk out the door, might also be "watching" and monitoring and patching fillings for the past ten years, and if presented correctly, these patients too, would want ideal dentistry. Not to mention, you would be able to buy the second practice for significantly less.

PRICE OF THE PRACTICE. The agreed upon price of a practice is the biggest negotiation factor. There are numerous other things to discuss however, before the deal is completed. This includes considerations such as financing, timing, accounts receivables, completion of cases in progress, cooperation of the seller towards writing a letter to the patients, and their agreement not to compete in the local market for a specified time frame. You never know if they got an offer down the street to work for corporate and decided to sell their struggling practice to clear some cash.

EVALUATE THE CURRENT SYSTEMS OF THE PRACTICE. If you are purchasing another dentist's practice, you might be purchasing another dentist's set of bad habits or systems that the patients were trained up with. For example, if the patients were used to paying only after insurance paid, or they had frequently allowed extended payment plans going on longer than three to six months, you might be having to retrain an entire patient base and staff on how you wish to run the business. If they had a casual approach to patients canceling appointments or strolling in late and still seeing them, you could be buying someone else's problems. In addition to patient retraining, you could be looking at staff retraining. Some doctors have a "hands off" approach because they don't like to confront problems early or in a timely manner and then the team starts making their own rules about coming in late, taking days off, or delaying certain uncomfortable critical tasks that should have been completed (i.e. making past-due collection calls).

K.   CREATING SOLID BUSINESS SYSTEMS

When you look at statistics, depending upon which criteria you use, a new (dental) business that is established as a franchise will have a significantly higher rate of success that one that is not (utilizing *franchise mentality*). Outside of dentistry, only one in three businesses will actually be in business within ten years. If it is a franchise, the number rises dramatically to three out of four. What's the difference? Franchises are based upon solid business plans and systems and checklists. For this reason, having solid business systems in place is one significant key to success. Having a good location and a solid business plan will almost guarantee a solid chance of success. According to Wells Fargo Bank Finance, they have less than 1% failure rate on dental loans. As dentists, we should be proud of that. They realize that most dentists are innovative and will continually push themselves until they meet their goals.

Examples of business systems include creating scripts for the staff on how to handle the most common questions received on the phones. Checklists are useful for Treatment Room Set-ups, Policies for Equipment Maintenance, Supply Ordering and Lab Case Management. They are also helpful for New Patient Exams, Treatment Planning, Hiring and Training Staff and Marketing.

When these systems are in place, it frees up the doctor to focus on providing a more innovative clinical patient experience.

With good business systems in place, a leader can use data on implementation and monitor results better. It makes it easier to manage staff and redirect their efforts as needed. As an experienced dentist, hopefully by now, you will understand and appreciate the value of "knowing your numbers" regularly. (The second half of the value of statistics is knowing what to do "with" those statistics once you get them.) Some common statistics that an office should be looking at regularly are:

1. Number of New Patients.
2. Number of Incoming Calls that Convert to Scheduled Appointments.
3. Monthly, Daily and Weekly Production and Collections.
4. Treatment Diagnosed, Presented and Accepted.
5. Accounts Receivable.
6. Office Overhead Monthly.
7. Office Net Monthly.
8. Number of Hygiene Days.
9. Hourly Production for Each of the Individual Clinical Providers.
10. Amount Diagnosed in the Hygiene Operatories, and per Dentist.
11. Adjustments Monthly (Discounts, HMO write-offs, refunds, etc.).

More on creating the Business Systems for Success in Section Two, Chapter Four.

L. PURCHASING YOUR OWN BUILDING TO PRACTICE IN

When you consider what happens to your rent money, (if you are planning on staying at a location for a period of 15-20 years), it often makes sense to consider purchasing the building. You will be your first tenant. Real Estate typically is always a good long-term investment as long as the location is good and the local economy doesn't take a targeted hit from one particular industry. When you sell your dental practice eventually, you can either choose to keep the building for residual income or sell the practice with the building. Dental practices that include real estate have higher limits on the amounts of loans available since there is actually stronger collateral in addition to an ongoing income-producing business.

M.   SIGNING UP FOR A PREFERRED PROVIDER DENTAL BENEFITS PLAN

The decision to sign up for a new dental benefits plan that offers to send hundreds of new patients to your practice should be evaluated carefully. My dad used to say, "If something looks too good to be true… check again." There are specific strategies that must be implemented to avoid having an influx of new patients on a reduced fee schedule pushing out your full fee patients farther in the schedule. If you are increasing your overhead to accommodate these new patients, either by adding an associate or adding additional treatment rooms or additional staff, the slimmer profit margin provided by these plans might outweigh the added expenses brought on by the additional patient load.

If both you and a cross-town colleague sign up for a plan like this, your patients might switch to the cheaper plan their company offers now and go across the town to see your dentist colleague. Then if you sign up because you just lost a bunch of patients, the same thing can happen with his patients – then you both are seeing more patients at reduced fees!

There is potentially a hidden disadvantage to joining a program like this later on in your practice career. Often the hope may have been to make more money by being able to "upsell" these patients to more expensive treatment (i.e. TMJ, sleep apnea or cosmetic dentistry, etc.) that isn't covered in their plans. Unfortunately, having a plan like this in your business can lower the eventual sale value of your practice by 10% - 15% in contrast to a comparable practice that is primarily fee-for-service with the same production numbers!

The business skills to make a reduced fee program work are different from those for developing a relationship-based referral practice. The clients are often less loyal and typically looking only to get the dental work that is covered under their plan.

N.   INVEST IN ADDITIONAL CLINICAL TRAINING OR ADVANCED EQUIPMENT

You could create more of a "niche" dental practice. By taking advanced trainings at one of the dental institutes to learn more comprehensive dentistry, sedation dentistry, TMJ treatment, holistic dentistry, sleep apnea, or dental implants. Some practices have been known as "boutique" practices, where they tend to cater to full mouth reconstruction or large cosmetic cases only and they market heavily in those areas. This can insulate you from the battle in the trenches for the emergency insurance-benefits-driven mentality patients. One of the problems with having a boutique cosmetic-driven practice, is that when the economy is down, many "elective" procedures get delayed. Plus, when you get around to selling, depending upon the niche you choose, buyers interested in that practice may be limited.

You could even take extra training in one or more of the specialties and just do more of a specific type of procedure (instead of referring that procedure out.) For example, you might learn more about treating the more complex oral surgery cases, root canals, or orthodontics and keep those in your practice rather than refer them out to specialists.

Often, the doctors who sponsor their staff for these seminars will have an easier time integrating them into the practice. Offering **Continuing Education** to your team helps them learn what you are learning. It shows that you are invested in their advancement as well. Moreover, many of the additional services beyond basic dentistry require a stronger involvement of the team to bring to full implementation. Unless a team member learned a particular advanced training at another office, chances are they were barely exposed to it in dental assisting school or front office administration trainings.

You could invest in a large piece of equipment such as a 3D CBCT imaging system (cone beam x-ray machine), a CAD/CAM milling machine, a digital scanner, or dental lasers and learn how to maximize your investment. Most of these newer technologies will support the growth of your practice by either assisting with your ability to diagnose better, explain treatment to patients better, save you time and money, or provide a better-quality service to your patients. Again, if you need to finance these types of equipment, most banks would consider them good solid investments with strong potential to increase your income and productivity.

O. RESTRUCTURING YOUR LOANS

If you still have Dental School loans, those are considered *unsecured loans*. Due to the high rate of failure on student loans, many loans are not as desirable to hold onto for the long term. Your tax benefit of dragging out your student loan debt is not what it was 30 years ago. This is especially true if you deferred payment on the loan due to a GPR or other additional training. If you own a home, sometimes consolidating your loan into a home-equity loan may actually afford you a lower rate, and the interest will be (currently) fully deductible. A loan on your home is a *secured loan* and banks prefer those anyways. You could even consider a home-equity loan as an option for securing funding for equipment that you feel is necessary for building the business and has a great chance of returning the investment soon.

P.   BEING DIFFERENT

Give people a reason to talk about you and your office. If patients perceive that they will get the same care with any dentist they pick, they will not be as loyal. Attempt to continually create new ways to set your practice apart, and let your patients know how you are different. This doesn't mean bragging about everything you do, but it can be subtle things like extra amenities in the bathroom, small personal gifts to those patients who refer friends or just completed a large case or are just a pleasure to work with. A few more ideas include holding raffles (using their appointment card as their ticket), having fun and decorating the office around the various holidays throughout the year, offering free whitening or cleaning for engaged couples just before their wedding, doing a "Halloween Candy Buy-Back" Program, and many, many other fun things for the patients to enjoy. Going that extra mile, one percent farther than the other dentists in a few dozen ways, can push your practice a long way. Teach your staff to put out that extra one percent effort when it comes to always leaving the patients feeling better about themselves after having been with you or to your office.

Q.   ESTABLISH SOME TYPE OF RETIREMENT PLAN

Most people start too late in their career to properly fund a retirement plan. They are more interested in today's activities and investments and debt. Even if you are only able to fund the plan with a small amount monthly, over the years, the compound interest from a tax-deferred earnings plan will provide you a significant benefit. Whether you decide on a IRA, a Simple IRA, a SEP IRA, or another type of profit sharing program, you should at least do something. Some plans are more expensive to set up and others are very straightforward and less costly. The biggest benefit of any plan is the timeline that it will be earning interest. Suffice to say that those who start earlier will have better tax consequences and long-term benefits.

R.   PURGING YOUR STUFF

If you are fortunate enough not to be a "pack-rat", congratulations! Many people collect way too much "stuff" that they will never need or look at again. If you integrate a new system and don't anticipate using the older system (whether it be a piece of dental equipment, an old stapler, a used cable, or a previous edition of a book that you just got), be prepared to purge it. As dentists, we get tons of magazines and articles and advertisements sent to us weekly. It's time to purge. If you haven't looked at it in two years, consider the relevancy of the information, the accuracy of the data, or the timeliness of the products. When something is sitting in your visible space daily that you will not be using in the near future, it's time to put it in storage, or better yet, sell it, donate it, or toss it. These days, a significant amount of the information for which we needed to hold onto older books and magazines can often be found online. If you aren't giving your office and work space a quarterly overhaul, ask someone to help you. They will be able to push you a little to get rid of things you don't need. The phrase *"opportunity cost"* means that if you have one thing, it doesn't allow you to have the other because you are holding on to the one thing. The same is true with "attention units". If you have clutter on your desk or in your office, your mind will always think that you are busy with things. Some people can function in a messy environment, but for the majority of people, not spending time searching for things, buying duplicates because you can't find the first one, or just having to filter out all the unnecessary "stuff" constantly can be tiring.

The same is true for your computer AND your practice management software. If you have 100 icons on your desktop on your computer, it might be time to bring in an expert to help you organize files and get you back on track. Then DEVELOP some new habits so that you aren't back in this condition once they help you dig out of your mess. It is time to purge old accounts that are inactive, delete patients that haven't been in for many years, and delete duplicate information and accounts that you know will never get collected.

In keeping with not letting things "fall through the cracks", you should set-up new systems that make sure any patients who leave the office without an appointment have set schedules for being called at a later time. Same for patients who walk out with payment plans for their treatments or insurance pre-estimates sent out. You must follow-up on them as soon as possible, because it doesn't get easier as time goes by.

S.   GETTING INVOLVED IN THE LOCAL COMMUNICTY

If you live and work in the same community, it's easier to get involved in the business clubs, or civic groups. Patients enjoy seeing their dentist involved in a community activity, charity, or supporting local sports at the neighborhood high school. Don't join and not attend meetings. Join groups that you enjoy and are willing to invest time in.

SECTION ONE

STAGES IN YOUR DENTAL CAREER

CHAPTER THREE

THE ADVANCED DENTIST

The word "advanced" doesn't always mean older, although it typically would apply to dentists who have been practicing over 25 years. Some dentists consider themselves as either "Advanced in Skills", or "Advanced in their Career". I've known dentists who are still practicing and are over 80 years old, and I've known other dentists who sold their practice and retired when they were in their 40's. In the same token, there are dentists who have been practicing the exact same way for the past 40 years and there are younger dentists who have taken every course available and purchased every "toy" out there.

Either way, this stage in your practice, you are thinking about what's next and how you are going to get there. You may be looking to cut-back your hours to spend more time with family or travelling or pursuing one of your hobbies. As such, you may either be looking for opportunities to lessen your responsibilities in the day-to-day operations of the practice, through either an associate or partner, or you may be looking for an exit strategy for full retirement.

One condition known as "burnout" is when people get repeatedly frustrated or feel like they are in a downward spiral and can't see a positive future, so they start thinking about retirement. They begin to feel that they aren't being rewarded for the effort they are putting into running the business and the stress of dealing with new regulations and staff issues and financial concerns start to build up. The physically demanding detail and clinically demanding aspects as well as running a business all takes its toll. You want to be careful not to let the practice go into a downward trend and then sell it at its lowest value. There are many options available to either "revive" a practice or transition so you successfully go forward maximizing your practice asset.

There are many factors to consider before taking this next step. At this time in the game, the wrong financial decision in either the way you structure your transition, how much you ask for your business, or even poor timing on the sale of your business, could be very hard to recover from.

Selling your practice too late, too soon, or even selling it to the wrong person, while still working there part-time and watching as they drive it into the ground, can all have disastrous consequences. In addition, once you have sold your practice, your income producing opportunities become limited unless you decide to go back to work part-time in corporate dentistry.

If you are a dentist who has had a long career in dentistry, you are at the stage that most people think about when they hear the phrase "Practice Transitions". There are as many options and opportunities available at this stage as there were in the earlier stages, however, *recovery from a bad decision can be more grueling.*

Dentists who are planning on retiring in the next 5 - 7 years should start planning ahead in terms of whether to hire an associate, and what type of associate they should be looking for. They would want one who could take over the practice when they finally do decide to retire. A dentist who is hiring an associate but not planning to retire for a while may just be looking for an associate for comradery, to cover for each other when on vacation, or to help share costs, or to allow the primary doctor to specialize in doing more of a particular type of procedure they enjoy more, such as implants, sleep dentistry, TMJ, sedation dentistry, etc.

If you bring on an associate dentist right before you are ready to retire and they are not trained in the areas of specialty that you were, that part of the practice will drop off and it will not be a wise investment for the younger doctor. In addition, if you hired a part-time dentist as an associate so you could cut back your hours and they only want part-time hours as well, when you get ready to retire, that arrangement might be challenging to "fit" the right buying dentist into.

One of your options include bringing on an associate and cutting back but maintaining ownership. This option allows you to maintain control of the income producing machine you spent your career creating and allows you free time. Another option is to sell your practice to another doctor and then work as an associate on just those favorite patients of yours. This could get challenging especially since you are probably not continuing to work on building the business and you are taking potential income away from the new owner. These types of arrangements, unless planned out carefully, often don't last for longer than one year typically.

If you really wish to continue working, but don't want to own the practice, you could potentially work as an associate in your own office or at a colleague's office. More than likely, if you sold your practice completely and wanted to work with a colleague, it would have to be a long distance away from your current office so as to not compete with your own practice. You would have to start fresh with new patients.

SECTION TWO

CREATE THE STRUCTURE FOR YOUR SUCCESS

CHAPTER FOUR

- BUILDING THE SUCCESSFUL ORGANIZATION

- LEADERSHIP / SYSTEMS / MARKETING

SECTION TWO

CREATE THE STRUCTURE FOR YOUR SUCCESS

CHAPTER FOUR

BUILDING THE SUCCESSFUL ORGANIZATION

Leadership / Systems / Marketing

Dentistry is the product or service you provide. Just like any business, without proper marketing, leadership and employee management or quality controls, along with monitoring the implementation of business systems, you have a recipe for failure. This is why franchises have a significantly higher success rate than most new businesses starting out. Their corporate headquarters has done a significant portion of the legwork to provide all the systems and marketing and monitoring and training for it to thrive.

The three legs that all businesses rest on are LEADERSHIP, SYSTEMS and MARKETING. If any one of these is lacking, the business will not thrive.

LEADERSHIP

One of the qualities of a good leader is that they are able to create a vision and then implement that vision through empowering their team. The vision contains the strategies that are implemented in any business. This means that a well-run business that has a vision of offering only top-quality products and services will only offer that. They should build a reputation for excellence. One example of this is that many car companies that want to capture both ends of the market by having two separate lines of products will create two different brand names to isolate the vision for each, while at the same time trying to capture two different types of clients. One is going after the high-end clients, while the other is going after those looking for more of an economical car.

In dental school, they taught us to be clinicians. They did not teach us to be leaders and motivators and business people. One of the strongest qualities of a good leader is that they embody the qualities that they are aspiring to see in their employees. They need to be able to coach their own team to success

Building a team to carry out the vision of the business can be challenging sometimes. Proper hiring protocol can potentially prevent the "wrong" people from getting into an environment and becoming toxic employees. Organizing solid training and development programs for each employee with adequate feedback and timely progress meetings will keep a team on track. Celebrating with the team on the "wins" is critical for morale and motivation. Most corporations will throw huge parties for their employees when they reach certain levels of success in their growth. There is a certain point in the growth of a practice where it is highly advantageous to develop team leaders to run different departments in your business. With proper guidance, training and clear expectations, staff can "drive" the practice to new levels. An office that is well-run and experiences lower stress will tend to be more profitable and have more staff that are accountable as if they owned the business themselves. Be willing to invest in your team and give them the opportunity to grow. Consider offering not just clinical skill training, but also business and personal growth opportunities to have them grow as individuals as well.

Most small business employers don't spend enough time training their employees. Training should be part of ongoing employment protocol to help staff keep up with the latest in technology, as well as providing quality customer care. There is a balance between micro-managing your team and giving them too much leeway and then getting upset when they fail to perform to the expected level. When employees understand the value of their individual contribution and are recognized for it regularly and specifically, they will be more motivated to continue their growth. Allow them to fail at small attempts to expand their area of control while keeping them learning. They need to know that you are behind them, and have given them permission to fail and will help redirect them appropriately. One common strategy for training is teaching staff "scripts" to use when talking with patients. While these can guide the conversation, they must be embodied through role playing and practice, and then you need to let the employee rehearse the script in their own words in the way they feel comfortable in (while still maintaining the objectives and achieving the same results.) If your staff doesn't feel comfortable following your script, for example: "It is a great day at Sunshine Dental. This is Suzie. How may I make your day amazing?" the staff should avoid sounding like they are reading off a script – because it will come across as that. They should practice your specific script a few times and then offer a close alternative script that they feel comfortable with. The point is, they need to BE with the patient and have a fun dialogue with them and get in rapport as fast as possible.

Good leadership also includes correct prioritization of activities. What you focus on throughout the day is where the energy in the practice flows. Staff need to know what they should be focusing on at specific times in the day. For example, if you give them a list of patients to call that haven't been in for three years to follow-up on, but the patient who scheduled for a two-hour visit this afternoon just canceled their appointment, they need to be able to correctly prioritize their order of activities. There are things that are important and there are things that become a priority and are urgent.

Train your network of support (your staff, labs, suppliers, vendors) to always work with integrity, and trust. Your ability to take care of others concerns is one of the other pillars of success. Make sure your staff stay in communication and learn to take care of each other. One skill that some employees seem to grasp, and others have a hard time with, is anticipating the doctor's needs. This could be anything from the staff having a pen in their hand when they ask the doctor to sign a prescription, or another example, setting up the room for the next step in a multi-step procedure as the doctor is completing the first phase. This takes time to learn, but once it is ingrained and systematized, it will make procedures go smoother and more predictable.

As a business grows, it becomes more and more important for the owner-dentist to focus on two things. The first thing to remember, is that the dentist's (and hygienist's) primary role in the office is producing the dentistry (which typically includes examining and educating patients). The more procedures and administrative support that the team offers to handle, the more profitable the business. Therefore, empowering your team through proper training, monitoring and feedback is critical to the success of any organization. An empowered team feels more satisfaction in their work. When the staff feel valued and appreciated and see the results of their efforts, they begin to take "ownership" of their roles in the practice. The goal is to develop leaders in the team as the practice grows, to take the day-to-day tasks and minor challenges "off the plate" of the owner. When offices have solid systems of accountability (monitors or trackers) and consequentiality (feedback) for the actions the staff take, it becomes a team effort. When staff understand the *purpose* that the business exists, all their actions will be geared towards either moving the business forward or holding it back.

If you are tracking results, you need to SHARE these results with your team. Every statistic you record can have value, if used correctly. If you are consistent in acknowledging others when the statistics go up and not just complaining when they go down, your team will be empowered.

SYSTEMS

A system can be described as anything that creates an organized relationship of multiple interdependent and interconnected parts. In his book **The Checklist Manifesto**, author Atul Gawande describes how checklists can help turn extremely complex business systems into easily managed protocol. Just as an airplane has a checklist of tasks they must go down, to make sure everything is replenished, closed up, and prepared before they take off, every business has a series of tasks that when consistently completed, will significantly increase the chances for a successful result.

In addition to setting things up to run smoothly, every business has their own set of *"predictable recurrent breakdowns"*. These can be considered as conditions that need to be addressed. For example, in a dental office, the predictability of an undesirable event taking place goes up when certain steps are not carried through. A simple example of this is as follows – A patient not showing up for a previously scheduled appointment. If you analyze what conditions were prevalent or steps that might have led to this, you can refine your systems for scheduling and confirming appointments in the future. If you were to schedule a family of four to come in for dental cleanings on a Monday the morning after they returned from a two-week trip to Europe, there are a dozen reasons why this is a recipe for failure. The planes could be delayed, one of the children could get sick and since they are traveling over the weekend; either have a hard time contacting the office to let them know, or when they get back, there most likely would be a pile of items on their desk for them to handle and decide to reschedule, since it's "just a cleaning" appointment. From this one example, it would be easy to brainstorm numerous options to ensure this doesn't happen in the future. The new systems to implement could be as simple as sending a confirmation email a week in advance, not scheduling a family the day after returning from a vacation, splitting up larger blocks of appointments to minimize the risk of one cancelling all their appointments, or other possibilities. The staff could probably even think of several other possibilities to handle this.

This same type of scenario can be applied to many other "flows" within the office, from making sure treatment plans are completed properly, to insurance information being updated, to room set-ups being fully done in advance before seating patients.

Offices that are constantly improving their systems will typically have less stress and more productivity in their business. Systems help to increase accountability in the staff and integrity in business. It helps to create a consistent experience for the clients. There is a program called **"Six Sigma"** that many larger corporations have embraced. One of the parts of their business management philosophy is a problem-solving system called DMAIC. This stands for Define, Measure, Analyze, Improve and Control. Every system in the office has a flow. Several examples of this include: How the phones are answered, how you present a treatment plan, how you follow-up on an insurance payment that doesn't pay what was anticipated, and to how to do a clinical procedure. Every step that can be quantified, measured, or improved in terms of quality result or speed of service is looked at and documented. Reducing the number of "negative" results, problems that can come up that can derail progress, and streamlining the result can create significant improvement in desired results and improve the bottom line of any organization.

Another area of practice management that dentists often have concerns over is the increasing *overhead* required to run a dental practice these days. Increasing your monthly production and making sure you collect what you produce, along with reducing cancellations are some of the first steps to shifting that ratio around. Producing dentistry without strong financial arrangements and letting accounts receivables get out of control can be a symptom of a broken system. Having clear protocol for ordering and keeping all the same supplies in the same place can prevent over-purchasing or buying an item and then forgetting where it is, only to find it two years later... and finding the product shelf-life has expired. Staff salaries are probably one of the biggest expenses on the books. Having productive regular meetings, effective bonus plans, clear job descriptions and strong accountability will assist in keeping these in line. Finally, having a high treatment plan acceptance and proper scheduling of patients will make a big difference on the bottom line.

It is critical that an office keep statistics on the *Key Performance Indicators (KPI's)* in the Practice as mentioned earlier in the book. While the staff don't need to know every single statistic you keep, they should be aware of those that they can impact as well as those that impact how you run the business and how you evaluate their support of your practice goals. These give reality to the actions taken and conversations had in the office. If the doctor wishes to earn $100,000 per month, but is only diagnosing $65,000 worth of dentistry each month, that will be an impossible goal for the staff. On the other hand, if the doctor Diagnoses and Presents $150,000 of new dentistry treatment plans per month and has a 75% acceptance rate of treatment, the $100,000 target is very attainable. Without knowing these numbers, you are just shooting in the dark as they say, and hoping for the best.

There is a process called "Reverse Engineering" with which you can determine what your typical overhead is, the desirable salary at which the doctor can pay their bills and have money for savings, retirement, and a little "buffer". If you know your ratio of accepted treatment plans (after having tracked it over a period of several months), then it's a simple math calculation to identify what your Bare Minimum Goal each month is. Setting up a bonus system for the staff that allows them to share a predetermined percentage of the profit above this minimum goal can help motivate the team and lets you know that if you are paying out a bonus, it is not coming out of your paycheck but the excess that the team and you earned. Regarding bonuses, there are certain times when it might be OK to base it on actual Production numbers. For example, if you are paying an associate dentist who works only part-time in a high-volume clinic that does a lot of write-offs, it could get confusing and complex as regards to dividing up and assigning payments to various family members' accounts and different doctors with multiple insurance write-offs or bookkeeping discounts that the corporate owners control and make decisions on. In general, for staff bonuses, it is always a good idea to base it on Net Collections, because if they schedule treatment but don't collect the money or have poor financial arrangements, the doctor cannot pay the bills with "production" money, only what came in through collections. Bonuses should also be fair for both the doctor and the staff. It may be tougher to evaluate effectiveness with daily bonuses as most offices will have some high production days and then low production days (for example, procedures such as seating crowns or delivering dentures or completing a root canal take time but don't have fees attached to them.) Any bonus system should be re-evaluated at least every six months or whenever the office purchases a large piece of equipment, expands the facility, or adds additional staff, particularly clinical producing staff such as another hygienist or an associate dentist. This should be openly and clearly discussed with the staff, with the understanding that if overhead goes up, so does the baseline for bonuses. This often helps the team weed-out non-productive staff as they will see that a particular employee is costing the office money and eating into their bonus money.

MARKETING

Marketing means a lot more than simply just putting up advertisements in a local paper or sending out fliers. It is a set of activities, communications, and actions that an organization executes to educate potential clients, convert them into clients, and keep them going forward. It happens via the implementation of the vision of the business alongside strategic actions that create desire, motivate, and provide solutions to people's problems. It educates people on not only the value of your products and services, but also on the potential cost of NOT utilizing your services. (For example, most people have been trained to take their cars in for oil changes every few thousand miles because they understand that if they don't, their engine won't run smoothly and therefore it's not a hard sell to implement).

Marketing does not begin once the patient comes through the door, it starts with how they found you, and is solidified and expanded during the first phone call contact at your office. If a patient tells their neighbor about you and how nice you are, or how you handled a complex situation, that's a version of marketing. When they call the office, if they are greeted by a pleasant knowledgeable and inviting person on the other end of the phone, that begins to solidify your reputation and integrity. The key is to get them psychologically involved. This means, asking questions about what may have prompted them to call. If it was an emergency, you can address the concern, if they are calling about getting their teeth whitened because of an upcoming event, that is psychological involvement. Engage in a brief conversation with them on the phone and dig deeper. Having someone on the phone who makes it sound like every call is an interruption to their day can destroy expensive marketing efforts to build a business faster than almost anything else. Since a large portion of your success depends upon the ability of the person answering your phone calls, it would be prudent to do call analytics and see how your marketing dollars are being spent. Recording calls for training purposes has become commonplace. If your front desk team are not converting a high percentage of your first-time callers into scheduled appointments, that is potentially an area that requires training. Call Analytics can tell you the source of your calls and give you a better idea of the conversion ratio. Placing a tracking phone number (sometimes referred to as a Dynamic Number Insertion, or DNI) on your external marketing can help you discover where your marketing efforts are paying off. When combined with Call Recording and Monitoring, all three can help provide you with valuable information and feedback for budgeting, training, and improving your marketing.

Presenting yourself as the authority on certain topics or in specific niches takes time and repetition. Being known as an authority in a specific niche helps create a level of trust through developing a relationship that is compelling and provides security to customers. This builds loyalty and protects a business from the advertising noise out there that could steal your clients away.

Marketing can be internal or external. *Internal marketing* typically doesn't cost much if anything at all. It could be before and after photos on the wall, it could be clean facilities and happy staff, or it could be clear persuasive conversations that the hygienist has with the doctor in front of the patient about their treatment. Internal marketing could be a monthly or bimonthly email newsletter that you send out to clients that updates them on your staff, your facilities, the continuing education courses you take, it could spotlight one particular patient and the benefits they got from your services, (including emotional benefit and personal confidence when possible). Internal marketing is every interaction that you have with your clients, from the way you answer the phone, to email messages, professionalism in handling patient concerns, and the speed with which you take care of things.

External marketing is more expensive, and not everyone who hears your message may be at a point where they need your services, or they may already have a provider that already meets their needs. Examples of external marketing include your website, your social media, yellow page ads, radio placements, TV ads, direct mail fliers, health fairs, news releases, and new mover marketing postcards. These may be targeted to your geographic or demographic market, but it doesn't mean that they are ready to hear your message.

These days, keeping up with optimizing your **website** and managing your web presence is not something most dentists should be attempting to do on their own. It has evolved into a highly specialized task that in today's market is best left to the tech-savvy marketing companies. To do it effectively requires several hours a week, which can be better spent providing patient care. Creating an effective website is a combination of skills such as being artistic, writing effective and compelling articles, understanding *Search Engine Optimization* (SEO) and being able to layout the material in an easy-to-follow format. Your website should be a reflection of who you are and the type of clientele you wish to attract. Having the "right" amount of appropriate graphics and videos will help let your potential clients get to "know" you better before they contact your office. In addition to being easy to use, your website should be informative as regards your procedures, let patients know about new equipment or procedures in dentistry and include some type of social media interaction either through videos, review pages, interactive links, and include a *"Call to Action"* offer for new patients. The Search Engines are constantly changing what they look at when ranking websites on the listings. If you are not on the first three pages of Google these days, you should not expect to receive significant referrals from the Internet.

One critical trend in the website business, is making your website *"mobile responsive"*. This means that the web pages are designed to be user-friendly and to display well on all devices, particularly smart phones. In the past, web designers would build two different websites and what showed up depended upon identifying what device you are viewing the site on. Now, the design of the site needs to be such that one site will work on multiple platforms and multiple devices. This also helps with Search Engine Optimization, since there is only one site that needs to be accounted for. As the number of people doing searches on mobile phones goes up, the more emphasis the responsiveness of your website—new, fresh, accurate, relevant, and technical information has become critical. Most people looking at a website on their phone are looking for the phone number (one button click-to-call), the address, directions, or to make an appointment, and the easier it is to do all that, the better.

Your ranking on search engines such as Google depend upon a number of factors, however, mobile responsiveness, and unique and frequently updated information are two critical items that will help you rank high. Other factors that are important include the loading speed of the website, the consistency of your name, address, and phone number (also referred to as NAP). Broken links and duplication of text, or the use of common stock photos from other web sites may actually hurt your rankings.

Another aspect of utilizing the Internet is maximizing your presence on Social Media. This means looking at having a solid, educational, fun, relationship-building presence on the WEB. It doesn't mean only putting marketing messages out there. It means letting clients and potential clients get to know you better and give them information that is not only educational but also fun and help them make better decisions as it relates to their health. The more interactive and relationship building your Social Media page is, the better.

Other examples of external marketing include: writing articles for the local paper, submitting a blog Online, or putting fun articles or pictures on Face book. External marketing can increase your name or brand recognition, and build credibility. Current patients might read about you or see something that you are involved in and appreciate that you are out there and being active in the community.

Both facets of marketing – internal and external, need to be carefully executed to give a consistent message about your practice. Some offices try to be all things to all patients, meaning that they handle all phases of dentistry. They handle high-end comprehensive dentistry and then they take every discount insurance plan out there. While this may be possible to pull off, it is an extremely challenging and frustrating option for the staff, because you will need to offer different levels of care to different patients, depending upon their financial situation. Changing gears is not that easy for most staff and can lead to confusion, particularly when families have different dental plans and different fees for the same procedures. When deciding upon how you wish to be known in your community, try to be consistent in your message. This is all part of marketing - a critical part of every business. The bottom line is, unless you are doing something in your marketing to attract attention, people will forget about you.

Quality control is another arm of the marketing department. If you survey your clients, you may be able to identify your own strengths and weaknesses and therefore put together a plan of action to strengthen or redirect your efforts to improve. There is a saying that "money loves speed". Many personal development entrepreneurs will claim that they invented that phrase, however, the essence of it is that people, especially today, have come to appreciate having the things they really want, "right now". They don't like to wait for results. If you can deliver a product or service in one day that someone else takes two weeks to deliver, and the quality is the same, and the price the same, (or possibly only a tiny bit higher), most people would go for the sooner delivered product or service. Part of this is because we have become a population of people that like instant results and quick answers. When you can provide this kind of information or feedback or correction, you will win.

Too often, after several years in practice, if the doctor is taking home a comfortable salary, they may tend to begin to let things go on "cruise control" and slowly, different systems start to fall apart as regular monitoring gets set aside. One of the best ways to give yourself a boost is to look at the following chart and do a self-assessment. Better yet, it's often a good idea to have an unbiased set of eyes look at the variables in your practice. Get a comprehensive exam done on your practice and look for those areas of the practice that may be out of alignment. When your vision outgrows your skills as a manager or leader, it's time to consider bringing in a coach to guide you to the next level in your business.

Someone who understand the DENTAL PRACTICE MASTERY MATRIX and takes the time to really focus on every aspect of it will reap the benefits of their efforts. Discover your strengths and weaknesses in each area and it will greatly assist with producing more consistent results in your business.

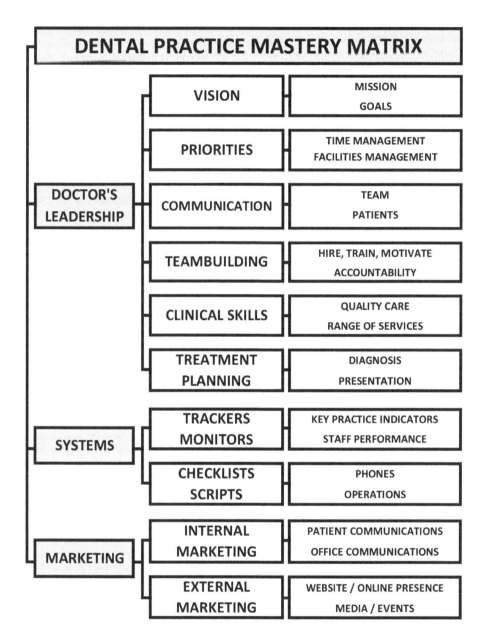

Fig. 1 Dental Practice Mastery Matrix

SECTION THREE

DENTAL PRACTICE BUSINESS MODELS

CHAPTER FIVE - SOLO PRACTICE

CHAPTER SIX - ASSOCIATESHIPS

CHAPTER SEVEN - PARTNERSHIPS

CHAPTER EIGHT - SPACE SHARING

CHAPTER NINE - BRINGING IN SPECIALISTS

CHAPTER TEN - SOLO GROUP PRACTICE

CHAPTER ELEVEN - CORPORATE DENTISTRY

SECTION THREE

DENTAL PRACTICE BUSINESS MODELS

CHAPTER FIVE

SOLO PRACTICE

If you choose to pursue a solo practice, which is the business model that the majority of dentists exploit when they decide to embark on their own, you can either purchase a practice or you can start "cold". If you build your own practice from the very beginning, and purchase your own equipment, design your own office layout, and order all the supplies – you are truly starting from scratch. According to the ADA, solo practices are still the most common eventual paths for nearly 80% of the new dentists. A solo practice has the potential to be the most rewarding path for people who are entrepreneurial in spirit.

As noted earlier, the number one challenge by the *economies of scale* (savings from achieving higher production numbers) afforded by the group practice option is shifting the thoughts of many new dentists as they graduate from school heavily in debt. Because of this, dentists who chose the solo practice model are required to streamline their offices for efficiency and systematize their practices to weather the ups and downs of local economies, in order to stay strong over their career. Many consultants are starting to suggest that in the years ahead, it will continue to get tougher for a solo practice dentist to compete with the potentially greater capacity and economies of scale that partnerships or group practices might be able to offer. Because of this, the demand for stronger leadership and business management skills are required of independent practitioner dentists.

Most solo practitioners work under a *"sole proprietorship"* business model. It is the simplest model tax-wise for an individual dentist. There are some tax advantages and economic protection advantages to becoming *"incorporated"*, however. When the business is incorporated, the corporation owns the practice and the doctor is on a salary just like the staff. Corporations pay taxes and the employees pay taxes as well. This makes the tax paperwork more complicated and often will require that a tax attorney help you. One common type of incorporation for individual dental practices today is an "S" corporation which offers some of the benefits of a corporation, but where simpler paperwork reporting is needed and many of the rules of sole proprietorship apply. There is also the Limited Liability Company - LLC option, which works not only for solo practitioners, but also for partnerships. They are the most flexible options from a tax perspective. Again, the main reason to look into the different options for a business entity is the desire to separate your personal liability from that of the business. Incorporating your business may not be something you need to do right out of dental school, but later in your practice, as you grow, it is a great way to protect your personal assets from any type of negligence or debts from the business. This is especially more relevant in a partnership situation. "Partners" are liable for each other's actions. Incorporating can limit your liability.

Depending upon your long-term goals with the business – such as, sell outright, turn it over to a family member, sell and work as an associate for a few years, or owning the building with the dental business in it – can influence which business model you should adopt. Because the taxation and structure and paperwork rules on these options are constantly changing and can be complex, a comprehensive evaluation of each is beyond the scope of this book. Therefore, we will limit our discussion to suggesting that you speak with an experienced small business tax attorney to find out the best option for your particular situation.

The key reasons that you should carefully decide if a solo practice is for you is that this model requires the highest financial investment needed to get going and the biggest managerial responsibilities for it to be successful. You will need to put a lot of time and energy into growing the business while improving your clinical knowledge, and all while being accountable for all your patient's well-being.

The primary reasons a dentist will go into sole proprietorship private practice is that they have more control over their own businesses and therefore have the potential for higher lifetime earnings. In addition, when it is time to retire, they would have built up equity in a practice – that they can sell, and use that huge asset as part of their retirement plan funding strategy.

Regardless of the route you choose, whether it is to purchase a practice, join a group, or start cold, one excellent habit you should incorporate early in your practice life is tracking your personal statistics. More on this is covered later in the book in great detail. If you start studying your numbers such as your hourly production, and your percentage of accepted treatment plans compared to what you presented to patients early on in your career, you can watch your progress as well as set realistic goals for yourself. This way you can feel more in control of your own income.

PURCHASING A PRACTICE RIGHT OUT OF SCHOOL:

If you choose to purchase an existing practice, then there are several considerations that you should be aware of. If you have a trusted colleague or advisor, they can help you research a practice before you jump into it, either as an associate or a buyer. There are certain ratios for procedures or number of staff, or days of hygiene, based upon the size and nature of the practice. Just because a dentist claims that they have 3000 active patients is a good idea to look through their appointment book, look at the number of days of hygiene, and the number of new patients they are getting each month to see if the numbers they are presenting match up to their claims. It is highly advisable to have an experienced advisor help you evaluate a practice, as a wrong investment could cost you hundreds of thousands of dollars.

BELOW IS A LIST OF SOME OF THE INFORMATION YOU SHOULD LOOK AT BEFORE YOU JUMP INTO ANY NEW PRACTICE SITUATION:

The size of the practice. Evaluate both in terms of number of operatories as well as the size of the active patient base. "Active patient" means a patient that has come into the office during the past 18 months, however, most people push it to 24 months, and in rural areas it could be 36 months. Some dentists who do "boutique" dentistry can survive under 1,000 active patients comfortably because they are providing quality comprehensive dentistry. Other practices can boast having over 3,000 - 4,000 patients, and still be marketing for more patients. This might reflect in each new patient's value to that practice.

The location of the practice. Is it a stand-alone unit or in a medical complex which may offer easier referrals compared to other medical professionals? Is it visible from the street, or will it depend heavily on advertising for people to find you?

The number of new patients the practice currently gets. Is the practice growing or plateauing? Looking at the number of new patients coming into the office over a period of 2 - 3 years by month can tell you if the doctor has "mentally" retired or is still promoting the practice. The same goes for Production and Collections Numbers.

Evaluate the current patient "load". Is there an abundance of patients or is the practice spending thousands of dollars each month to attract new patients who typically come in but don't stay?

The source and number of new patients monthly. (PPO's vs. walk-in vs. referrals vs. discount advertising) If patients are primarily from discount advertising, you may find that a significant number of them are not with the practice after 12 - 18 months. This is referred to as "the back door being as big as the front door". In other words, they may be getting a lot of new patients, but these are not loyal patients. Rather, they are patients looking for the cheaper cleaning and exam fees, so they will leave for the next advertising dentist in town. Referrals from loyal patients will always be your best source of new patients. They are already pre-sold on you as a dentist and will typically consider you their doctor from the start. If the practice participates in HMO's or PPO's, you should review all their contracts to see the last time they renewed them or updated the fee schedules for those plans.

Are the selling dentist's current fee schedules in line with the rest of the community? If they haven't raised fees in years and you come in and raise them all at once, that could trigger an exodus of patients, especially if it is not shared tactfully and professionally with the patients.

Why the dentist is selling their practice (Retiring, cutting back, injury? etc.).

Whether the staff will be staying (Often, keeping some familiar faces will encourage those patients who drive a longer distance to stay.) It would be good to have a list of all the staff and their dental histories of employment at the practice and local areas, including any benefits or unusual fringe benefits the office might offer. Also check to see if the office has a high turnover rate on employees or difficulty in hiring new people.

Does the practice have solid Financial Arrangements they follow for Treatment Planning Cases? If they don't have solid financial arrangement policies, and patients are allowed to make up their own payment arrangements, you may have a challenge shifting them to a more responsible policy. Retraining both the staff and the patients could take time.

Whether the dentist will help with the transition by introducing you and completing the involved cases that they have been working on. This is important as it helps to carry on the goodwill of the practice.

The types of procedures the office provides. For example, if they were offering sedation and dental implants, and you have not been offering either of these, you may have a harder learning curve, or may not be able to reproduce the same kinds of results that the previous owner was, in their niche practice.

The ratio of prophies to perio recall and root planning appointments. If they do not have an active perio department, or an overly aggressive one, then the ratio will be off. Do they refer a lot of perio therapy out to specialists or do they actively treat them in the practice?

The personality of the exiting doctor. For example, are they outgoing and extroverted and you are introverted and quiet? If your personality is completely different, it could either turn off or offend some patients who might be used to a different style of practice. This ties into the CULTURE of the existing practice. Is it upbeat and fun or business-like and quiet?

The outstanding debt currently with the practice. Did they recently purchase any large equipment and currently have ongoing debt that will be transferred? Will they be paying off any current debt on the practice? — this is ideal.

Whether the office space is leased or is part of a real estate deal included in the practice. If the practice also includes real estate and has other units adjacent, you will become a landlord, and it adds an extra dimension and potentially more stress but potentially a bigger payoff long-term. This requires a different skill set than being a dentist. If it doesn't include the building, you need to confirm that the landlord will offer a reasonable lease rate for an extended length of time to make it worthwhile. If the landlord needs to raise the monthly rent due to the area becoming more valuable (such as a large corporation buying up all the local properties), you need to lock in a reasonable rate early on.

Is there room for expansion to add another operatory or merge with an adjacent office? If you decide to add an associate in the future, a 2 - 3 operatory office might be challenging.

Evaluate the amount of local competition with similar businesses. Are there a dozen dentists within walking distance, and if so, will the density of the population support that. What is the ratio of dentist to population? In some urban locations, there could be dozens of dentists right next to each other and they are all busy, whereas in more rural areas, 2-3 dentists will be competing for the local business. Talk with local dental labs, dental suppliers and bankers about the success of the existing dental practices.

Potential for growth from procedures the prior dentist did NOT handle, but may have referred out (such as orthodontics or oral surgery or root canals). Look at the mix of procedure codes that the current dentist performs. Are there procedures the seller referred out that you like to perform or can do to keep it in the practice? This is good, it allows room for growth.

Look at all the statistics that have been kept for the practice. One useful statistic is the ratio of "Accepted and Scheduled Treatment" to the new "Diagnosed and Presented Treatment". If the current dentist had a significant amount of treatment that was presented but not scheduled, there could be a big potential opportunity to provide that additional dental care to the patient base. If that statistic is either too high or too low, it could be a function of the ability of the dentist to present, or diagnose treatment or it could be a matter of their fees being too high or too low.

The age of the equipment. Will you be needing to upgrade the computers, the chairs, x-ray units, etc. If you need to purchase new equipment you should consider it when negotiating the price of the practice. Look to see the last time that they purchased a large piece of equipment.

The demographics of both the dentist and the neighborhood. Obviously, in certain areas of the country, it could be an issue if you are not similar looking or speak the common language.

The Accounts Receivables Report. It would be useful to assess the financial policies of the practice and see how much is over 90 days. If you are newly out of school, you may have higher needs for payment at or before the procedures are delivered. If it was an older practice and all the patients were used to being billed for everything and made payments as needed, they may not like your stricter financial policies.

The right to do a LIEN search on the practice to see if there are any outstanding debts against the practice that were not brought up.

Do a web search on the Doctor and the practice. Check on Google, Bing and Yahoo, as well as social media such as Facebook, Yelp, etc. Learn about the practice's personality and reputation online.

Study the Adjustments Report. This report will tell you if they are offering significant discounts to friends, family, seniors, colleagues, or insurance companies. Production Numbers only give one side of the equation. If there are significant discounts being written off each month, this can also tell you the nature of the business.

Look at the practice Attrition Rate. *Attrition* is the gradual reduction in the active patient base over time. It is the number of patients leaving the practice each year. This can vary between 15-30% or more per year, depending upon the location and the type of practice you have, and the patients you attract. In other words, if a patient comes in to see the dentist, are they still in the books with an appointment one year later? An attrition rate of higher than 50% for a practice after 18 months is a red flag. If they are heavily marketing the practice or aren't managing the new patient experience or the staff well, the high attrition rate can be one symptom of that. The office is missing out on the opportunity to build long-term relationships with their patients. That is what adds value to a practice.

Hang out in the practice for a day or two. If this is a place you plan on spending a significant amount of your life, it makes sense for you to actually go and observe the dentist working for a day or two to see the flow and study the systems they have for carrying out the various procedures. Some owners may NOT want the staff to know that they are considering selling or making a transition until it is about to happen. This could potentially trigger them to leave or cut back their loyalty on referring, particularly if the staff know that the owner is about to sell the practice.

Quality of the Dentistry provided. Take a look at the crown preparations that the current doctor sends to the lab, look at x-rays of completed work, ask about any warranty they offer their clients on work done. If you purchase the practice, are you purchasing the warranty, and if not, how is that to be handled?

Currently, with the market as it is, BANKS are willing to offer very good loans to both new and experienced dentists for acquiring dental practices. Obviously, a dentist with good credit and a few years' experience would qualify for a higher amount plus some working capital as opposed to a fresh graduate coming out of school. In addition, they would be more likely to risk a higher amount on an ongoing practice that shows solid growth for the past three years versus a brand-new practice with no history of income.

Dentistry and Medicine have low default rates and the banks will do what they can to help out a dentist in the unlikely event that they hit a slow few months in a row for whatever reason. As of 2017, purchasing a dental practice is still a good investment (for banks) and if there is real estate involved, the banks are even more interested, as traditionally, real estate will appreciate in value. You can anticipate a range of 65 - 80% of the last three years gross collections average when determining the price of a practice. Obviously, there are several modifying factors, but this is a starting point.

When looking for a bank to help fund your loan, it is always a good idea to look for one that offers industry specific type loans. This is different from a typical "collateral-based" loan. As regarding these types of loans, banks look at your collateral, such as your home or your car to secure the loan. Banks that offer dentistry specific type financing will offer "cash-flow" loans. The loans are typically structured to allow you time to earn the money over 10 years or more and use your cash to keep your business running. As mentioned before, the dental industry has a good track record and therefore, a bank that specifically offers healthcare practice type loans will generally be more flexible and offer you lower interest rates. They will even work with you if you let them know about an unexpected short-term business disruption that might mean taking a brief break on making payments to get back on your feet.

GETTING READY TO PURCHASE A PRACTICE:

Once the decision to purchase a practice is made, whether you are a new dentist or an older dentist wishing to expand their practice by acquiring another dentist's practice, there are certain things lenders will want to see before lending you money. In addition to the obvious, such as a license to practice that is clean, they will look at your CREDIT RECORD, current outstanding debt, and overall monthly expenses. If you have a large mortgage and a vehicle loan payment, other personal debt, such as back taxes or alimony and are a solo practitioner, you might not qualify for as much as someone with a lower mortgage, no other outstanding debt, and a great credit score. In addition, if you are married and your spouse also has a good income, they can be added as a guarantor onto the loan and it will allow you to qualify for a higher loan amount. Getting your personal finances in order is a good prerequisite for getting a quicker loan approval. If you have a decent down payment, the banks will also look favorably on that. While you can't "pre-qualify" for a specific loan amount since the amount would depend upon both the practice statistics as well as your financial history, you certainly can have things "lined up" to increase your chances of success.

As mentioned above, just like when you purchase a home mortgage, a commercial small business loan rate may vary, or the amount may vary depending upon your Credit Score. In order to get the best rates and structure for your loan, you should be sure that you have been paying your bills when due, staying below your maximum credit limits, making sure that you have some savings set aside for a slow month—so that it doesn't affect you whether you can pay your bill that month or not, avoiding filing for a bankruptcy at all costs, and never let a debt go to collections against you. This will help provide you with the best opportunity for optimal financing. Try to avoid making any other larger purchases, for example a car, a home, or large appliances on credit right before you are looking to apply for a loan for the dental office.

Finally, when you are considering acquiring a business loan to finance your practice acquisition, in addition to having a good credit score, it is always a great idea to have a solid business plan in place to show your lender how you intend to grow the business and be profitable. While loans may be easy to get, the banks still want to see a good business sense in the person requesting the loan and if they understand the flow of money and taxes strategies.

STARTING A NEW PRACTICE VS. BUYING AN ONGOING PRACTICE

There are many advantages to purchasing an ongoing practice vs. starting a completely new practice. Specifically, there already is momentum going, and income coming into the practice, which makes it more desirable to a lender financing your practice. While the upfront costs may be a little higher, when financed over time, it will allow you to have a quicker return on your investment. Generally, there will also be several business systems already set up, allowing the business to have a flow of patients, people and paperwork, already established. Obviously, when you purchase a practice, over time you will implement your own systems but the ongoing practice will at least already have some type of structure in place.

A practice that is ongoing will give you about two years head start over one that you start from scratch. The only difference is that what you consider the actual amount you pay initially for the practice is not the final cost. You must evaluate all the factors mentioned earlier, and the age of the equipment. For example, if you will need to upgrade most of the equipment in 3 - 5 years, keep that expense in mind. It is going to take a considerable amount of marketing to get a practice from scratch to build up the same momentum. Generally, it is considered that a dentist takes 2 - 3 times longer to get to the same production levels if they started on their own, as they have to hire staff, purchase equipment, and set up all the systems from scratch.

In addition to putting together a team, facilities, and equipment, you will be spending a lot of time doing tasks like:

(1)   Getting a Business License,

(2)   Registering with the Drug Enforcement Administration (DEA) so you can write prescriptions,

(3)   You need to get your license from the State Dental Board, and register with them,

(4)   Register your X-ray Equipment,

(5)   Sign up for a Radiation Safety License,

(6)   Find a Payroll Service and an accountant to help with quarterly taxes,

(7)   Secure Professional Liability Insurance (malpractice insurance),

(8)   Get Workers' Compensation Insurance and put up all the appropriate posters and signs,

(9)   Create an Office Injury and Illness Prevention Plan, and numerous other requirements,

(10) Hire a Dental Office Waste Disposal company for hazardous waste,

(11) Get set up with a Merchant Account at the bank and secure a Credit Card Processing machine. These are just some of the many tasks to complete when sorting out a start-up. (This list was partially compiled by the California Dental Association website - www.CDA.org)

When you start from scratch, you have the opportunity to hire and train employees, set-up all the business systems in the practice, market the practice, and get all the procedures and equipment and supplies in order. The time it takes to do this eats into clinical time and therefore you need to have a supplemental cash flow (*working capital*) to support you for several months. While it is potentially more satisfying and rewarding in the long run, it is a riskier way to begin your career.

STRATEGIES TO CONSIDER WHILE INVESTIGATING A PRACTICE TO PURCHASE:

There are CLIENT RETENTION STRATEGIES. When you purchase another dentist's practice, a significant portion of the price is determined from the current active patient base and the assumption that they will stay with the practice to provide you with the same income levels. While this is ideal, it is not realistic. This attrition can result from any number of reasons. Patients may stay if you get into relationship with them quickly and build trust. These patients had a longstanding relationship of trust and friendship with the previous dentist and if you critique the previous dentist's work they might not trust you and leave. If they travelled a long way to see the dentist, they may decide to change to a closer dentist, since now they will have to find a new dentist anyways. If you are too rough or too aggressive, or too young or too old, if you are of a different race, religion, sex, or nationality, it might be enough for them to leave. Since this is common with any practice transition, and since dentistry involves a close personal relationship with your patients, you must put together a strong strategy to either incentivize patients to be willing to "try you out" and give you a chance to earn their trust. Among some of the strategies, include a sincere letter of appreciation and support from the selling dentist describing how they already pre-screened a number of candidates and chose you. Since they trusted the selling doctor, they should also trust in the selling dentist's judgment in selecting the buying dentist who will take excellent care of them as well. Other strategies would include having a going away party, and an *introducing the new dentist and patient appreciation party* to allow the patients to get to know you, and at the same time say goodbye to the old dentist. Finally, having a video or nice pamphlet made, introducing you and spotlighting your training, experience, and the skills that you will be bringing to the practice.

MAKING SURE THAT YOU HAVE PLENTY OF WORKING CAPITAL ONCE YOU HAVE SPENT YOUR FUNDING MONEY ON PURCHASING THE PRACTICE. If the practice takes a dip in production during the initial few months of the transition, you must not only be able to cover the overhead, but also have extra money to do additional marketing for the practice to bring in new clients. This is referred to as *working capital* – that is, enough money to cover the daily expenses of running the business. If you need to ramp up external marketing due to a decline in business, it can get expensive quickly.

EVALUATING REALISTIC OVERHEAD NUMBERS. There are typical ranges for the various fixed and variable expenses in a dental practice. When evaluating the list of expenses for a dental practice, you should dig deeper into them as some of the expenses might not carry over to the new owner. Items like Dues, Insurance, Automobile Expenses, Legal and Accounting Fees, Continuing Education Costs, Travel and Entertainment can vary significantly from one doctor to the next. If the selling doctor was writing off everything possible, it might make the overhead look higher and the profit margin lower for the potential buyer, which is good.

Depending if the practice does more of one type of specialty services or if they have a CAD/CAM machine it can shift the overhead numbers a bit as well. It is a good idea to know what is considered typical and get solid explanations for numbers that seem out of the range of typical for a practice like theirs.

SECTION THREE

DENTAL PRACTICE BUSINESS MODELS

CHAPTER SIX

ASSOCIATESHIPS

An *Associateship* arrangement occurs when an owner-doctor hires another dentist to work in the practice. The Associate is usually hired to assist with the clinical procedures of the practice and does not typically have any upfront investment nor significant managerial responsibilities. Associateships can be a useful tool during the life of a dentist, especially when the desired outcome and five-year plan works out as anticipated. They offer the associate doctor an opportunity for additional experience without a large financial commitment. The owner-doctor can often benefit from leveraging their facility, their team, and their resources, while adding the flexibility of potentially taking more time off, having shared coverage for the office after-hours, along with the opportunity for some passive income. In addition, an associate can assist with a transitioned phase-out to retirement for the owner, or they can do the 'bread-and-butter" dentistry, while the owner-doctor specializes and focuses on a specific aspect of dentistry that they truly enjoy. In this section, we will take a closer look from both perspectives.

WORKING AS AN ASSOCIATE IN PRIVATE PRACTICE

An associate position has certain options and benefits that purchasing a practice outright doesn't offer:

These may include a steadier, regulated income and immediate income without financial issues or long-term commitments. Typically, an associate experiences fewer headaches than one running a practice and dealing with all the local labor laws and government regulations that business owners are responsible for implementing and carrying out. Working as an associate has typically fewer after-hour emergencies (unless that is one of your duties). You could potentially pick up and leave for another city without much deliberations. Associate positions often have a lot more flexibility in scheduling. You can take personal time off (3 - 6 months) to have a baby, or travel and not have the financial concerns of your practice falling apart.

If you chose to take the DENTAL ASSOCIATE route, then here are some things to make sure that you are a valuable associate. To increase your value at the practice, you should attempt to include some of the managerial responsibilities of running a practice. In addition, you can take an active role in helping with reactivating some of the older patients who have been with the practice but just need a nudge or a little special offer to have them back at the office. You can mention some new high-tech tools or special training the office now provides that the older dentist may not be familiar with or wanted to offer (such as dental implants, sleep dentistry, etc.). Once you get into the practice, you need to quickly determine how much time each procedure requires and challenge yourself.

If you are considering purchasing the practice in the future, you should make provision for that eventuality in the contract so that there won't be a misunderstanding later. In addition, while you are helping to build up the practice for the owner, you might end up paying for that additional growth by adding value to the practice, if you haven't addressed that in the initial contract. It is a good idea when hiring another dentist as an associate, to have the office "appraisal" done. That way, in the future, should the discussion of the associate either buying into the practice or buying the entire practice come up, you have a starting point. The second critical item to put in the initial contract is a restrictive covenant. In the event of death or disability of the primary owner, without a restrictive covenant in the contract, the associate has strong bargaining power, according to William P. Prescott, E.M.B.A., J.D. in his Winter 2008 Quarterly supplement to his book, **Business, Legal and Tax Planning for the Dental Practice Second Edition.** Although the associate could purchase the practice, there is nothing keeping them from setting up shop across the street and soliciting all the patients he knew or treated instead.

Most associate dentists are hired in one of two ways: An associate can be hired as an *employee* of the dental practice or as an *independent contractor*. As an employee, they would be subject to having income tax, Social Security and Medicare withheld from their checks, whereas, if the associate had an independent contractor status, the office wouldn't pay the taxes, but rather the associate would be held responsible for making those payments. For all practical purposes, the work they do is the same, however, the legal and tax liabilities would be different. As an employee, you would have access to Employee Benefits such as medical insurance, vacation and sick pay for example. As an employee, there are also labor laws and state and federal guidelines that need to be observed. Pay periods and tax consequences, and worker's compensation needs to be carefully considered. As an independent contractor, employment laws and labor laws do not apply. You would be responsible for handling all your own benefits and tax responsibilities.

The classification of an associate as employee or independent contractor should be considered carefully, since the government imposes penalties and fines for improper classification. For more information on determining whether to set up your arrangement as an independent contractor or an employee, search on the **IRS.gov** website, or you may use this direct shortcut (**goo.gl/KxTpjt**). There are three categories of rules to help determine the status:

> (1)   Behavioral Control,
>
> (2)   Financial Control,
>
> (3)   Type of Relationship/Benefits.

Whatever arrangement you set up for the associateship, you should always have an experienced employment attorney familiar with small business law review your contract before you sign. One or two missing details in the contract can cost you significantly more than the few hundred dollars you saved by hiring an inexperienced attorney. Because independent contractors have to cover their own taxes and they know that you don't have to pay benefits, they will often ask for a little higher compensation. In most cases however, *it is advised to have an associate listed as an employee* to avoid potential issues with taxes.

Being an associate, while offering some flexibility and easier entry into dentistry, has some drawbacks. Associates often will get the less desirable work shifts (evenings or weekends), the less desirable procedures put in their schedule, the less profitable procedures, and use the older equipment. They don't build up equity in the business working there, unless it is pre-arranged that way. They don't often have much say in how the business is managed.

HIRING AN ASSOCIATE DENTIST:

If you are considering hiring an associate doctor, there are several things in addition to finding the right personality and skills that you should consider. One is the timing, and another is the reason that you are considering getting an associate. Earlier in your career, you might consider having an associate for the *camaraderie*, or you might want someone to come in and perform certain procedures so you could focus on those other procedures that you enjoy more. Or, it could be for the purpose of gaining little freer time to pursue other things, or possibly for emergency coverage, or in case of personal family emergencies that might take you away from the practice. Later in your career, you may rather desire someone to "take over" the practice as you retire. If you get the "wrong" person in there at the wrong time, just because you like them as a person, it could become a costly financial disaster or result in a legal issue as you go about trying to correct the decision.

Sometimes, dentists experience a few weeks in a row where all of the sudden they are super busy and can't see a patient in a timely manner. This is more of a scheduling challenge than an "I need an associate" challenge. Remember, once you hire an associate, you are responsible for providing a livelihood for them. If someone joins your practice and then after the initial rush and backlog is done, and you've been spending time training them and held back on marketing, you may find all of a sudden that you don't really need an associate. If you had hired an associate, at this point, you would have two dentists that you need to ramp up the marketing for, in order to keep you both busy. If you don't have a proven system for increasing patient flow on demand, you may find yourself in a bind. If you "feed" the associate your patients because of guilt or to try to keep them from leaving, you will soon find yourself in a negative cash-flow situation, since the associate's salary is going to be increasing the overhead.

Doctors considering hiring an associate should consider one other thing. While one of the goals is to free up some time for the owner, there is the trade-off of typically LOWER net income for the owner. The office production may go up, but so will the overhead. Sometimes it can take up to one year or longer for the owner to get a return on their investment in the associate. The practice needs to have a strong marketing program ready to instantly supply double the number of new patients to keep both the primary doctor and the associate busy. Without a new inflow of patients, what often happens is that once they see all the current patients who were backlogged (waiting for times to schedule their treatment), there may be a drop in the production.

You should have a growth strategy in place to empower your new associate and mentor them into the business. Too many offices hire someone and then let them fend for themselves. Just as you wouldn't hire a staff member and not train them, the associate dentist must be part of the team training as well. With that in mind, many consultants suggest that the associate get full access to the most experienced assistant to help them get up to speed. In addition, that assistant might be able to subtly "coach" the new associate along on certain materials or equipment as they are working together, helping to maintain confidence with the patient.

Now that you have done the internal practice analysis and have determined that it would be appropriate to hire an associate, there are several places you can look for associates. Ideally, if you knew someone looking whom, you had a professional relationship with or who worked with a trusted colleague, that might be the first place to start. Placing ads in the journals and with the local Dental Society is helpful. Asking your dental supply reps and dental labs can also be a great source of potential referrals. Once you find one or more that you are considering, it's a good idea to meet with them again, perhaps in a social setting with spouses just to get to know their personalities a little better.

When you begin to consider hiring an associate, there are several things you should consider and/or discuss with them first:

1. Does your practice have the patient load to support two dentists? Generally, a single dentist can handle between 1,200 to 2,000 active patients comfortably. If the number is between 2,000 to 3,000 active patients, then you might be ready for an associate.

2. Do your office facilities have enough space for another dentist to work unencumbered? If you will be working at the same time, three operatories is probably too few. Four to five operatories, while being tight, can work if you plan on splitting hours somewhat, and 6 - 8 operatories would allow tremendous growth for the practice. If your original facilities are small but you have the opportunity to expand the facility, then that might also be OK.

3. Will the new associate be bringing any patients with them or will you need to do all the marketing to keep them busy? Have they ever done any marketing for patients and what has worked?

4. Is this new dentist someone you would enjoy hanging out with if you weren't in practice together? You might want to go out to dinner with the dentist and their spouse, if they have one, to get more of a social interaction feel of the new dentist.

5. What skills will the new dentist be bringing to the practice? What areas of interest do they have that will complement your skills?

6. Are you looking for someone to cover your emergencies after-hours?

7. Are you looking for someone to help with management responsibilities? What responsibilities relating to supervising others did they have at their prior offices?

8. Is the position one that will evolve into a partnership or a buy-out in the future?

9. Why are they leaving their current position or situation?

10. What are their expectations from you in terms of growth within the practice?

11. Will you be hiring the additional staff to work with them, or will they? Do they have any experience hiring and firing or training team members?

12. What happens if one of you wishes to take an extended vacation or needs to take time off for medical or family reasons?

13. If they are hired, what benefits will they be entitled to? (Paid vacation, continuing education, sick days, personal time off, holidays, medical and dental care, retirement plan, etc.)

14. What special financial arrangements will be made if they work on family? How far does the definition of family extend? (Aunts, uncle, cousins, etc.?) If you pay on production and the patient receives a senior discount, which amount will be credited for the work?

15. You should discuss your philosophy on the type of practices you wish to build, whether it is focusing on high quality individualized comprehensive dentistry or high-volume production-oriented practice. If they are "used" to being in one of these environments, are they interested in changing or do they prefer the former. (It's not as simple as saying that you want to offer *high-fee, relationship driven, comprehensive care* if you were used to high-volume, fast-paced, insurance-driven care.)

16. How do you handle it when the new associate really wants to get a new expensive piece of equipment, but you don't, and don't agree that it would be beneficial financially to the practice, HOWEVER, if they DO get it, you would utilize it?

17. If for whatever reason, they wanted to leave the practice, how would you decide what "sweat equity" they may have developed to build up the practice. This should be clearly defined in the Initial contract and it should NOT start until after the first year with you.

18. How connected to the geographic location are they? Do they have family nearby but it is just too far to drive? (Would they stay if something happened to a relative they cared about that lived over 500 miles away and needed help?)

19. How do they solve problems when it comes to either a dispute in the way an employee was handled, or a patient being treated through their partnership?

20. Ask them what types of courses or books they study or read that are non-clinical.

21. Find out if there are certain procedures they enjoy performing and which procedures they'd rather not have to perform. In a similar vein, is there a certain aspect of running a practice that they don't like or feel they are good at?

22. Find out if they have any seasonal or extreme sports hobbies that take them out of the practice frequently.

23. Find out any other outside family, or religious commitments or obligations that they may have pre-arranged.

24. Find out if they are interested in doing hygiene exams, and if so, you will have to determine if there is a percentage of an exam fee split.

25. Ask where the associate will be living? It would be nice if they live close-by so they can attend to emergencies or be involved in the local community.

26. Find out if they are familiar with your computer practice management system and any high-tech equipment you may use. It is important to get them trained as soon as possible.

27. Look out to see if they have a bad credit record or any prior incidence with the State Board.

28. It might seem obvious, but it's a good idea to ask them their ten-year goals. Sometimes they might be thinking about moving out of the area but didn't want to tell you, if you didn't ask.

29. Finally, the uncomfortable question: What are their anticipated income goals working at your practice? (This should actually be one of the earlier questions, when you feel comfortable, as it might eliminate a lot of unnecessary questions if they have unrealistic goals based upon your particular style of practice.) You don't know what they were earning before or are capable of producing until you ask them or check their references. Unfortunately, in many cases, you don't have the luxury of asking their references because they might be their current employer! You can also ask them about their minimum income levels to cover their expenses in the event that the business slows down.

Realize that if you are a practice owner LOOKING for an associate, there are a few common reasons why someone might be available and looking for an associateship. Either they are new and they aren't as confident in their clinical or business skills yet, or they have external pressure from finances or family and they don't have the resources of time, money, or energy to start their own business. Another possibility is that they aren't very good at selling themselves when talking to patients about treatment and they need time to build that confidence up. Finally, they could be moving to a new location and just wishing to work only part-time without the added burden of owning a practice.

Many people state that associates aren't as committed to the practice, and if you turn over a portion of your practice to them, they will most likely drive it into the ground. But if you are willing to mentor them and they are willing to be coached, there is a *better* chance of success. You can't just hire an associate and not expect to coach them or guide them towards becoming successful. The more energy you put into making sure that they are as active as you are in developing the business, the more successful they will be. In addition, there is a concept called "sweat equity" in which an associate can earn a financial interest in the practice. This is favorable if the associate becomes interested in purchasing the practice down the line. For example, if they worked there 2 - 3 years and built the practice up through of their efforts, the practice would have a higher value. They shouldn't have to pay "again" for that added value, therefore, with sweat equity, they have an opportunity to put aside an additional 1% or more each year into a separate account that can be applied to the eventual purchase. On the other hand, should they leave the practice, they leave that money with the practice, because it is potentially a significant disruption to the business to have associates coming and going. It would be a good idea to not have them earning sweat equity immediately upon starting. You want to confirm that they are a good match for the practice first.

A significant number of doctors who bring on an associate into the practice will be open to some type of buy-in after a proven track record of care and integrity. Once they see the value of an associate and the commitment they have made, it is likely some type of arrangement to advance into ownership will follow. There should be a time set up at the beginning – being a date that you identified in the future, that assuming the associateship is doing well and you both wish to pursue either a partnership or a buy-out, is scheduled for a practice evaluation assessment. The new associate doesn't want to be building an empire that they will eventually have to buy back.

If the associate feels that they like the facility but that they have differing ideas on running a practice, they could also evolve into a *solo-group practice model* where they split up the patients and the associate gets to own 50% of the practice by themselves. More on this is covered in a later chapter. This could have benefits over having two owners and possibly a split loyalty of the staff to one doctor or another. If the purchase of the half of the practice is done in installments, it's even more challenging, because the primary owner-doctor will want to maintain executive decision control over the business until the payments are completed. One of the big personal challenges to owner-dentists when they convert an associate into an owner position is the loss of total control over the practice. There are now two mindsets running the business.

Another situation that arises from time to time is where the associate doctor is given a compensation package with an initial *percentage earning deal* that is "too good" or overly generous because they are really wanted. When they are offered a higher ratio of collections than the owner is getting, there would be little to no incentive to becoming a partner or owner. They would actually be earning less if they did buy into the practice! In the long run, yes, they would own a part of or all of the business, but for many years, they would see that option as not favorable to transition into. Why would someone pay an associate more than they calculate their own overhead is? Two primary reasons. It is common that they may be looking for a long-term colleague to share ideas with and expenses and emergency coverage. Secondly, it is assumed that the "fixed expenses" of the business, such as rent, equipment, electricity, etc., will not go up. Only the "variable expenses" portion of the business, such as supplies and lab bill and possibly support staff will increase as production increases.

Regardless of what the original intention of the associate is when you are having initial discussions, you should always include some type of "restrictive covenant" in the contract along with a clause that states that they can't "steal" your employees should they decide later on to set up shop down the street. If there was a mutually agreeable separation of the associate and the primary doctor, you could include some type of reasonable buy-out of the goodwill they brought to the practice, especially if they live and are active in the local community. In a case like that, enforcing a restrictive covenant to practice 20 miles away might be challenged or not be enforceable. This brings up the additional conversation about letting the associate in *too close* on the details of running the practice too soon. If they get ambitious enough, they may decide to take all your great ideas and go across town to attempt to duplicate your success, thinking that they don't need to give you any surplus income generated.

When determining what percentage should be paid to an associate, you can talk with local reps and other doctors to get a starting point. The bottom line is, the owner-doctor should be bringing in between 5 - 15% profit from the associate to cover additional administrative costs and for providing the initial capital for the office as well as the added management responsibilities that come along with having an associate.

Depending upon the geographic location in the country, the additional benefits allowed and the arrangement to cover supplemental expenses could comprise an additional assistant, an additional front staff, laboratory costs, continuing education, marketing expenses, insurance, etc. While paying an associate on collections is probably fairer to the office to make sure that all they produce are collected, the paperwork trail and splitting fees when there are prior balances and hygiene and insurance and discounts and refunds makes this a potential nightmare. Paying on collections is the fairest way, but paying on production is simpler and generally easier to account for. Most of the time, the ratio would be a little higher if you pay on collections, since that is the actual money brought in. There still is the question of compensation when working on patients who are fee-for-service vs. those in an HMO or PPO plan.

When hiring a specialist (associate) to work in your practice, the fee percentage paid out can be a little higher because their overhead is typically lower. In addition, if they are part-time, they will not want to be paid on collections if there are patients in your practice that you are providing them to work on. They don't have the time or resources to be tracking down insurance payments or compiling insurance checks when dual insurance or collecting becomes an issue. Therefore, it is more common that specialists hired into a general practice are paid a set daily amount of a percentage of production.

If you have an interested associate who is asking for a higher percentage than what you were willing to offer, ask them if they would be willing to work at the percentage you were offering and give them 4 - 6 months to "prove" their value, with a bonus in six months based upon specific criteria being met. This will give you adequate time to see if they can produce at the levels you wanted and diagnose and promote the practice with an ownership mentality. Whatever arrangement you set up, it might be a good idea to re evaluate it in 90 - 180 days to make sure it is working for both parties. If you share your original intent of earning a small portion of what they generate for providing them the patients and facility, they should be reasonable when you ask them to lower the percentage a couple points if it is not working financially for you as the owner. In addition to doing a review with the associate, it would be good to include some type of incentive bonus program going forward. Again, this could be evaluated periodically and be based upon their contribution to the practice, the quality of the work done, the lack of re-makes or repairs needed on their work and their overall volume of production. As they work more efficiently, they could have a tiered payment plan that offers them an additional couple percent if they hit a minimum production goal in a certain time frame. You wouldn't want to do it based on a daily goal since it could vary radically day to day and that would discourage an associate from doing exams and other *lower paying* procedures. Rather, it might be on a monthly or quarterly basis that you re-evaluate their average daily or hourly production. If your personal production goes up because they are handling more of the simpler procedures and freeing you up to handle more advanced cases, that is also valuable as well. Therefore, it is good to consider the above criteria when looking at the office production numbers for both of you.

Another option instead of paying the associate the full percentage they are asking for is that, they could get paid a percentage of the total revenue increase for the practice as a bonus. This motivates them to do anything that will bring in income to the practice regardless of who handles it. They can perform hygiene exams, they can recement a temporary crown, and it helps build an owner-mentality into the associate. If you are able to produce more, there is a value to that and they can get a small percentage of the opportunity for you to be able to do more productive things. For example, if you wanted to focus on sedation and implants (assuming you enjoy performing those procedures) having the associate handle pediatric treatment and composites can free your time up for the more productive services.

Another factor you should look at when hiring or coaching an associate is reviewing a potential treatment plan they present to a patient. It is important that they have the practice philosophy, the same as yours – the owner. Are they over-diagnosing or under-diagnosing? If so, going to a comprehensive treatment planning course together would potentially be valuable. In addition, in the early days of the associate at the practice, it is a good idea for them to "shadow" you for a couple of days to see your style and the flow of the practice, so patients can get a more consistent feel when or if they should see the associate.

Another reason to re-evaluate things in 6 months is that it will also give the associate time to determine if this is the right practice that they would be willing to commit to for a long-term. During their time at the office, they will probably be talking with their buddies and finding out what other offices are doing and what the going pay structures are. This kind of information could either solidify or destroy their motivation at the practice. Therefore, it is a good idea to invest time in training and helping them be successful in your practice. It is an expensive and awkward phase in a practice life if you need to undo an associateship that isn't working for either party. It is important to review your mutual goals and those of the practice periodically.

Having an overpaid associate long-term could be an issue if you ever wish to sell the practice and the associate wants to stay but not buy the practice. Anyone looking at purchasing the practice might not want that associate, either at that rate he is paid or at all even, which could affect your sale as the owner of the practice.

Be careful about over-promising too much to the associate, especially if you just met them and don't truly know their work styles and how the patients and staff like working with them. Limit conversations about buy-ins or the specific value of the practice until after you have been able to evaluate the speed, skill and personality of the associate.

TERMINATION CLAUSE. There should be some type of clause that discusses how the associate contract should be terminated. Life happens, businesses evolve, economies go up and down, opportunities present and people change their minds. Insufficient patient flow, staff conflicts, health issues, and practice management differences are just a few of the reasons associateships dissolve. Most associateships will either evolve or dissolve within five years. Knowing this, you should plan ahead for how the associateship will terminate, and document that in the initial contract agreement. There should be a suggested time frame (30 - 90 day written notice) to allow each side to *regroup* and take care of their personal needs during the transition. If you decide early on that this is not the "right" associate for the practice, you should let them know quickly, as the longer they are there, the more confused newer patients will be who their dentist is, and the more the staff will be disrupted. Unless there is an "unfriendly breakup", it is important to discuss these things in advance. There should also be a strong covenant not to compete in the contract when discussing termination of the arrangement.

More on hiring or working with **specialists** as associates is covered later in this book.

SECTION THREE

DENTAL PRACTICE BUSINESS MODELS

CHAPTER SEVEN

Partnerships

A partnership can be a powerful business model if you find someone with common goals and complementary strengths. Some doctors may prefer handling surgery and other doctors are into technology or Involved Comprehensive Restorative Care. If you have a partnership and share patients, having different clinical strengths can offer options to your patients. In addition, some people might find certain personalities more compatible. (Similar to how some patients might prefer one hygienist over another.)

You want to have a solid vision for your business before signing a partnership agreement. There are basically two versions of group practices and then multiple variations within those models. It could be two dentists working together sharing one facility, one set of staff, equipment and patient load. Or, it could be two or more primary owners who bring in associates working in a larger GROUP PRACTICE business model. Under this model, sometimes, there are multiple facilities in different cities or different parts of the community. When the doctors have different skill sets or if they merged two practices to create one entity but with multiple facilities, it can work well if the original practices were doing well to begin with. If one is struggling, you don't know if that is because of poor business systems at the office or local factors contributing to that office not thriving.

In the multiple facility model, there should be one primary care dentist to be accountable for the success of that facility. It could also be a strong office manager, but typically, it would be a dentist. This is because offices develop personalities. People become loyal to those personalities. If there is no consistent personality, there is no loyalty. Patients come and go for whatever reason.

In a multi-location partnership, if the doctors float from one location to another with the intention of bringing a specialized skill set to that office, that is OK, because the primary doctor has conferred confidence in the incoming dentist to the patient. Some example of these more specialized skills include sedation, dental implants, TMJ, sleep dentistry, orthodontics, etc. Patients may not appreciate that it takes a LOT of energy and time to be an expert in ALL areas of dentistry and they will be OK with you bringing in an expert who has more knowledge in these areas than you. Because of the options for a professional team of dentists offering the care, patients may gain more confidence. As a result of this, more and more dentists are considering the group practice model for dentistry.

Two common challenges of group practices include personality conflicts and differences in management styles. Often, when two practices merge, there is one doctor whose management style is more laid back that the other. Their "risk aversion" might be higher than the other doctor. Since staff often take on the personality of the owner—one set of staff might be slower to adapt to new ideas on patient care, treatment philosophies, and employee involvement than the other.

In addition, one of the Doctors might be more lenient on enforcing staff employee policies (for example, personal time off, cell phone use, overtime, etc.) and this could cause a split in the loyalty of the staff to one doctor versus the other, potentially causing an internal strife among the staff. It can be difficult having two bosses putting different tasks on your desk, especially if you only have time to complete one of them.

Some doctors like to jump on every new opportunity or latest technology, while others like to wait a few years and let the hoopla about the latest gadget settle (until all the bugs are worked out). This is more evident with computer-type high-tech products on the market today. Sometimes, they become obsolete in a few years or they come up with a newer, smaller, more versatile version and the first one is not upgradable. One example of this is the 3D ConeBeam X-ray units. These amazing tools are becoming almost invaluable to every procedure in dentistry. If you had jumped on that bandwagon between the year 2003 - 2006, you might have spent between $250,000 - $300,000 or more for a unit. Currently, there are machines available for less than one-half to one-third that price that can do more, have updates added to them, and have upgradable software.

How this applies to a partnership is that if one of the doctors like all the new technology and utilizes it, but the other is reluctant about buy anything that they don't absolutely need, there could be a conflict. In addition, splitting up the costs and overhead of a practice can sometimes be tricky.

One doctor might use more technology and the other might work more hours in the practice. How do you split up revenue or overhead fairly? These are all questions that should be discussed before you sit down to sign your agreements.

If one of the doctors is considerably older than the other, then you should also write up how the partnership will be dissolved. It is similar to preparing a pre-nuptial agreement – but for business. When all the details of how the partnership will dissolve are written out with all the possible options, it makes the transition period less stressful and significantly less costly.

By doing your due diligence on the other business and doctor, you can potentially save yourself a very expensive break-up. "Due diligence" is a phrase used to describe making a reasonable effort to comprehensively look at the other person's business from a legal and accounting, and liabilities perspective, but also from the perspective of their clinical strengths, managerial practices, growth philosophies, and long-term goals.

In a group practice, there is also the potential for increased liability over the actions of your partners. This includes not only malpractice liability, but potentially also financial debt and business liability as well. For this reason, as mentioned earlier, it is a good idea to talk to your tax attorney about the best type of dental corporation that you should form.

In a solo practice, if you choose to purchase a piece of equipment or try out some new products, you simply purchase it. Bringing on a partner means that you now need to explain all your miscellaneous purchases and justify your major expenses.

One additional concern over partnerships is the valuation of the business in the event of one partner wishing to leave. Not only is it difficult to sell a share of a partnership, but finding the right doctor to come into the practice who can afford to buy it could be challenging. The other option is trying to have the other partner buy out the leaving partner. There should be a clear path and agreement on how to handle splitting up the patients if the leaving doctor wants to relocate nearby. There is also the discussion of who the staff would work with if they had been working with a specific doctor.

Partnerships have many of the benefits of a group practice such as sharing emergency coverage, camaraderie, being able to focus on different aspects of dentistry, sharing large equipment costs, and the potential for higher income due to sharing costs.

Many consultants will warn friends about joining to create partnerships. This is based upon the lack of long term successful partnerships, thereby ending a friendship as well. This is particularly common when one partner has limited business experience, or has a struggling practice when they came together.

If the two partners are more experienced and willing to agree on many practice goals and they are willing to support each other's continued success, then this arrangement might have a chance. Identifying the value of a practice while going into a partnership might be challenging if one has a lot of high tech equipment already and a larger practice to begin with. Everyone thinks that their practice is worth more than it really is, typically.

Another challenge that will come up when the partnership dissolves is: How do you determine who a patient belongs to? Especially if they walked into the office on their own without a referral and happened to see both doctors for different procedures. This is another reason the growth of the partnership as well as the original agreement should be periodically evaluated, updated and modified as needed to come up to par with the current situation.

It is always prudent for each party in a partnership to have separate representation from experienced attorneys to protect their assets and create an equitable and fair contract.

One other consideration is, eventually, as one of the doctors will need to cut back the number of hours or days they commit to the office – when this happens, they most likely would want to either add an associate or pay less percentage of the overhead. There should be something in the contract that addresses this issue.

When naming a business partnership, you may want to consider the future. If you think you may want to eventually add more associates or sell the practice, it would be easier to transfer it if it bears a name that is relatively generic or includes the location of the practice, rather than simply the names of the principal owners.

Finally, other potential areas of conflict can include when one doctor has their spouse involved in the practice, particularly in a managerial role. This could be a bit awkward for the other partners when trying to have specific tasks completed but the spouse is tending to prioritize or implement their spouse's ideas.

While it is impossible to predict all the different scenarios that can be encountered throughout the lifetime of a business, running a responsible objective evaluation of the person and all they bring to the partnership is wise. It can mean the difference of hundreds of thousands of dollars in the future.

SECTION THREE

DENTAL PRACTICE BUSINESS MODELS

CHAPTER EIGHT

SPACE SHARING

In this model, the facilities overhead is shared between one or more doctors. One doctor could be having extra room in their facility that they are under-utilizing and so they allow another dentist or specialist to rent that space, either on a daily basis or a production basis or a combination of both. Generally, you wouldn't see each other's patients, although for emergency coverage, it would be convenient since you occupy the same office and the patients are already comfortable going there. It is similar to a "Solo Group" model except that there is just the sharing of fixed overhead related to the facilities alone. This model also works well for specialists since they often need a larger geographic base of patients to draw from. We have seen instances where two specialists who have smaller practices in different locations, might "rent" space to the other specialist and they can expand their reach to attract more clients, particularly if they are not in the same specialty. (For example, an orthodontist and an endodontist or a periodontist.)

The overall concept is that there are two completely separate business entities that split the cost of the facilities based upon the idea of keeping their overhead costs down. They could even share staff, however, this often is not the case. Note that a Space Sharing Business model is not the same as a partnership or an associateship. You have NO contractual responsibility to treat or even see after hours emergency patients for the other doctor.

Often, a facility is underutilized. This means that one or more rooms could be used on days when they aren't seeing patients. For example, if there are open treatment rooms during the week, they could offer the space to another dentist or specialist to work out of. Generally, they don't overlap schedules, although, if they are compatible and there is enough space, it could also work that way. More commonly, one person might shift their hours and work evenings and weekends, for example. Or, they could work the days the other office is closed. This cuts the overhead costs down and limits the liability of each doctor because they are not in a business partnership. It can allow a dentist who wishes to work part-time the option to utilize a facility at a very low start-up cost.

It could be convenient if the doctors sharing the space use the same phone number or answering service, or answer each other's daytime phone calls, and that way, they will portray the office as being bigger than it is (by being open more days and during more convenient hours). By being available with a live, warm, friendly voice on the phone during more hours, it gives both offices more growth potential. This however, is NOT the case in the majority of the situations. They are two businesses sharing a facility. That is it.

This arrangement portends lower risk and higher reward when you can find a convenient arrangement like the one just mentioned, particularly to the renter. There is some risk to the owner that the renting doctor might not have as strong a commitment to maintaining the equipment and supplies. This could lead to frustration to the staff, if Monday morning arrives and the owner-doctor's staff see that the operatories are not restocked, or are left a mess because the other office staff had to run out of the office quickly at the end of their day. As long as there is a clear agreement for keeping up the facilities, it could be a somewhat financially rewarding option for both parties.

While this arrangement may work for a certain time period, often it does not allow for significant growth options or ideal retirement practice transition strategies due to the facility's limitations and the structure of the business. A dentist looking to buy a practice typically wants their own space rather than to share with another dentist they don't know. As a result, these types of arrangements are frequently used as transitional arrangements when primary facilities are being built or they are checking if there really is a market in that area for their specific type of dentistry.

When you sign your agreement, if it is with another practice of similar nature (i.e. two specialists, or two general practice dentists), you might want to put a clause in your contract that if one doctor wishes to retire or move, that the other person has the pre-agreed upon first option to buy their business. You can periodically meet to reassess the value of each practice, avoiding long drawn out legal issues if the spouse has other plans for the practice or they want to shift the business to another dentist office, thereby disrupting your business. Again, you have to remember that in a space-sharing arrangement, you are not partners. You shouldn't assume that just because you both have similar practices the other person will want to buy your business if you retire. If you had been taking care of each other's patients over the years, a prospective buyer would rightly be concerned that the patients would assume that you were in a partnership. They might switch over to the other dentist if for whatever reason the patients are not attached to the buying dentist or if the new dentist wanted to relocate the patient base to a different building.

The bottom line is, the space sharing arrangement for a long-term situation may not save enough money to compensate for the lack of autonomy and added potential of staff conflicts or maintenance of equipment and trying to come up with equitable sharing of maintenance costs. The bulk of the fixed expenses will still be there including all of the variable expenses. For purposes of building up a business with lower overhead, this practice model can function well. But for purposes of building a business to sell or transition out of, there are many things that should be taken into consideration first.

SECTION THREE

DENTAL PRACTICE BUSINESS MODELS

CHAPTER NINE

BRINGING IN A SPECIALIST

Patients will often appreciate the convenience of having a specialist working within your practice. While they have trusted you to care for them for many years, and wish that you could do ALL their dentistry, there are times when it might make sense to turn over certain procedures to someone with a little more experience in a specific area. The most common specialties or services offered by mobile specialists are: Sedation, oral surgery, endodontics and orthodontics – where they offer their services in a general practice either on a regular basis or on an "as-needed' basis. The time this will work well is when you have a very busy general practice and are frequently referring out treatment that either you should be handling or that you would like to see handled in your practice. If you are a specialist and you aren't fully busy in one practice, it is common to join a group practice and either work part-time or lease a space or office that isn't being used full time and work out of that facility from time to time.

Specialists typically have a different ratio of overhead than the traditional general dentist. As a result, the agreements with specialists are different from those with general dentist associates. While malpractice insurance may be higher due to the fact that they often deal with the more complex cases, their lab bills tend to be significantly lower (with the possible exception of a prosthodontist), and often their marketing expenses are typically less. A specialist usually markets to a general dentist, but if the general practice is busy enough, then that practice can support the specialist, typically part-time.

If you have a busier practice, you can afford to pay a higher percentage to the specialist. Typically, in addition to increasing your office income significantly, they also can often add a new source of revenue that you were referring out before. It is not a matter solely of you handling less dentistry to keep an associate dentist happy, it is about you keeping the procedures in the office. To the owner-dentist, this will also mean a higher salary overhead for the practice, but if you keep them busy when they are there at the practice, it will almost always be a win for both parties.

If you are bringing a specialist into your practice hoping that other local dentists will refer their patients to the specialist at your practice, you can let that thought go. It might happen on rare occasions or an emergency, but in reality, a general dentist will not send patients to another "general dentist" who has a specialist working out of their office close by. This is because of the potential for any side remarks about the condition of the rest of their mouth or work that you could also have done for them. There is also the risk the patient will start coming to you to complete all their work. In addition, they might report back to their friend, their current dentist, that you tried to let them know that you could have done it better or cheaper or faster at your practice.

Unfortunately, this would be true if you had a 3D CBCT (Conebeam x-ray) or any other resource "their" dentist doesn't have. They simply will not refer patients to you, because you are the competition.

SECTION THREE

DENTAL PRACTICE BUSINESS MODELS

CHAPTER TEN

Solo Group Practice

A Solo Group Model is different from a partnership in that you have two separate businesses. You share facilities and possibly some overhead, major equipment costs, with potentially a shared lobby and front desk area, and possibly even some shared employees.

In this model, both doctors are free to conduct their businesses as they wish. Typically, they will share the fixed overhead of facilities and major equipment, but supplies and lab bills are completely separate.

This arrangement offers many of the benefits of partnerships, group practices and space sharing, without the complications of business management styles, staff personality conflicts or loyalty and motivation.

Essentially, for this model to work well, there should be a large facility and you should divide up the hours for each doctor to use the facilities. If there are enough treatment rooms, you could overlap schedules. If there is limited space but you both want the same days, you could have one doctor start early and work six hours and the other doctor work a later shift. Or, you could share a day you both book your larger cases so that you don't need two to three rooms, but rather, you are working on only one or two big cases those days.

Each doctor hires and creates their own support team and treats their own patients, controls the treatment offered, and the method of delivery. Each office would have their own marketing, their own management styles, and their own array of procedures.

You can divide up the overhead based upon time in the office, amount of production, number of treatment rooms used, initial ownership of larger pieces of equipment, or any combination of these.

With the pressures from insurance companies and larger group practices utilizing *economies of scale* to offer lower fees for their services, this is one way to maintain your autonomy and yet have many of the benefits of a group practice.

Sometimes when a solo practitioner hires an associate doctor, over time, they like the facility but realize that they have different philosophies on management or patient care. The associate can at this time purchase half of the practice and begin to create two independent practices under one roof. There should also be an option to have the first right of refusal to purchase the other doctor's practice should they decide to leave the practice on retirement, disability or other reasons. Typically, the original owner would have the priority to purchase the practice back from the previous associate. When an associateship turns into a solo group practice, it costs the associate a significantly lesser amount to get into full ownership of a practice.

While specialists could have this type of arrangement, either a partnership or space sharing arrangement might be better options for two or more different specialists who wish to be sharing a facility. Their practices are run significantly differently than general practices and their overheads are different.

Additional considerations when entering into a solo group practice should include looking at the ages of the owner-doctors (and considering potential retirement options of one or the other), potential expansion of the business down the line, potential relocation of the business and options on buy-outs and or the possibility of becoming an employee of the other in the future, working part-time.

SECTION THREE

DENTAL PRACTICE BUSINESS MODELS

CHAPTER ELEVEN

Corporate Dentistry

Corporate Dentistry has a completely different management and treatment delivery style and focus than the solo group practice. Corporate dentistry is in the category of GROUP PRACTICES, as opposed to the solo practitioner model. Dentists who adopt this model tend to try to deliver and be all things to all people. Typically, these types of offices will have several doctors, often in multiple locations, running extended hours, sharing of patients, and working with patients who tend to be either heavily motivated by insurance maximums, or have lower incomes and are on a budget.

The number of multi-unit dental firms with 10 or more locations has grown five-fold between 1997 - 2007 according to the ADA. This trend is expected to continue, particularly because it is driven by the heavy financial burdens that many young graduates bear upon completing school (and looking to get into a paying job as soon as possible). They want to get out of debt rather than take a risk opening a new business and trying to compete clinically, and often don't have the cash flow economically to compete with the marketing budgets of big corporate dentistry. If this trend continues, within ten years, a significant number of dentists will be in some variation of a group practice model.

In addition, if a new dentist is looking to start a family, and be able to take time off, the corporate or large group model has advantages. The other doctors in the practice can pick up the patient load. If you run a solo practice, and wish to take off 2 - 3 or more months, it's almost financially impossible. When you add on the minimum costs today of starting up a basic brand-new practice at the range of the low end of $300,000 or with all the latest technology running into $500,000 - $700,000, it's no wonder many younger dentists are looking at corporate and group type options as viable options to kick off their careers.

A Dental Service Organization (sometimes referred to as a Dental Support Organization or DSO) can be disguised in many forms. Sometimes, they will offer to purchase your practice and give you all their management support to allow you to simply provide the clinical aspect of the business. Sometimes, older dentists get tired of running a business and opt for this type of arrangement. The DSO offers business management and administrative support to dentists, with the intention of helping minimizing their costs, and thereby offering lower charges to patients. It tends to be more popular in areas where there are underserved minorities or lower income populations who don't have as easy access or resources for adequate dental care. Typically, this model works best with larger group practices which can offer the opportunity for collaboration and learning. This is also great for new Dentists who don't feel that they have the speed or business knowledge to run a business. It can be a simple option for those dentists who still enjoy providing dental care but are interested in working only part-time without the additional financial burdens of owning a business. There are a significant number of females joining the dental profession each year and if they are considering starting a family in the near future, this can offer another attractive option to them as well.

The other type of support generally offered to these practices is in the area of computer technical support, staffing, payroll, legal assistance billing, and marketing. In other words, the dentist can put more focus on patient care and less energy on the non-clinical day-to-day demands of running a practice. Both the dentist and the team can often have access to additional benefits such as paid time off, license reimbursement, professional liability insurance and healthcare benefits. The cost alone of having these purchased individually can add up to a significant amount.

A DSO needs to be differentiated from "Traditional Private Practice Dentistry", in that, with the DSO model, the dentist is basically utilizing one source for all their non-clinical needs. In other words, the accounting, collections, human resources, dealing with insurance companies, tax preparation, payroll, etc. are handled by one organization rather than needing multiple people to handle that aspect of the practice. In Corporate Dentistry, their objective tends to be focused more on generating money and a higher volume and faster speed of delivery of service. Corporations have shareholders who want to see profits. Because of the untapped potential in the dental industry and lack of business training that most dentists suffer, many capitalist investors who are non-dentists saw an opportunity to jump into the field. They often have the business acumen and wisdom for creating teams and they understand effective management systems. As a result, they often have the capital to market more aggressively and offer volume pricing which makes their offer more competitive.

Considering that each dentist is different as regards to family and personal demands and external influences, this model may offer a dentist more flexibility in schedule and lifestyle. Because there are typically multiple doctors at the practice, this model offers dentists who adopt it more freedom on their evenings and weekends as they "share" the after-hours emergency coverage. It is also potentially a good model for a new dentist with debt coming out of school who needs to focus on earning money and has less experience with managing people and running a business.

On the other hand, as mentioned earlier, in a corporate setting, a dentist loses their autonomy and some flexibility. It requires a different management style. Because there are often many people working in the office, there is a higher chance of internal conflict arising between staff members. Plus, there is pressure on the dentists to produce. If you are forced to see 15 - 30 patients a day, some of the methods that help to build a solo private practice might not work as well. For instance, a good practice builder is to call patients the evening after difficult procedures. While this is not impossible if you see 30 patients in a day, it can potentially be challenging to remember all the patients and get in touch with them. With a small private practice, the focus is usually more on the "relationship" that the patients build with the dentist, rather than the convenience of the office hours or the fact they accept the patient's insurance plan.

Due to this higher volume of patients seen in the corporate setting, it is challenging and and potentially "not-profitable" for a dentist to sit and spend a lot of time building relationships with each and every patient and finding out about them and their goals for their mouths. They generally aren't given the time to do that. In addition, trust comes from building a relationship, so in the corporate setting, the loyalty of patients is not as strong. Because of this, when it comes to having dental work completed that is "beyond their insurance limits", patients often default to the mentality of waiting until next year to complete treatment or only doing what is covered by their plan. Patients are not aware of the potential consequences of it actually costing more or being more difficult to perform a procedure if you have to split it up over one to two years. If they wait until it hurts or turns into an emergency, then they may become motivated to come in. As a result, conservative, prevention-oriented dentistry that is outside the coverage plan often gets delayed, pushing the treatment towards more expensive, and more costly options down the line. Sikka Software did a two-year study (ending in 2016) of 12,500 practices and found that the typical dentist in a group practice did nearly twice as many amalgam fillings as a dentist in private practice.

This is generally because the group practices attract the HMO dental plans which pay out less than traditional benefit plans. In addition, the group practice dentists did about 15% fewer crown and bridge procedures than solo practitioner dentists, again, mostly because the dental plans accepted by the group plans did not pay a significant portion of those fees, patients often choose the cheaper restoration.

Dentists opting for this type of practice should know the following: In an HMO plan, the patients pay a lower monthly premium, but they are typically assigned a specific dentist within the plan—referred to as "in-network". The dentists stay on a specified fee schedule that has little room for negotiation. From the patient's perspective, there are often higher annual benefits and low or no deductibles. In the PPO option, patients can select their own provider – there is a deductible and an annual maximum. The dentist has a little more input on the fees, but the insurance plan still only pays a percentage of the fee. Typically, they would save more money if they went to a dentist who is "in-network" – which means that they usually will accept the lower negotiated fee schedule.

One final word about Dental Support Organizations (DSO) group practice models is that they handle all the regulations and governmental compliance issues in advance, this makes joining one of these programs more attractive in some way. In addition, they do all the insurance plan negotiating for you so you don't have to deal with completing insurance paperwork, or payroll for that matter.

As discussed here, it takes a certain type of personality to both run a managed care corporate practice properly, as well as work in one. Dentists who have worked the sole proprietorship model for the majority of their careers are used to certain freedoms and liberties that might not be available in the corporate model. As a result, it tends to attract the younger dentists who are either aggressive and wish to go into management or those who simply wish to have a "job" as a dentist.

SECTION FOUR

RETIREMENT TRANSITION STRATEGIES

CHAPTER TWELVE

- BUILD YOUR PRACTICE WITH ASSOCIATES

CHAPTER THIRTEEN

- SELL YOUR PRACTICE – WORK AS AN ASSOCIATE

CHAPTER FOURTEEN

- SELL YOUR PRACTICE - RETIRE

SECTION FOUR

RETIREMENT TRANSITION STRATEGIES

CHAPTER TWELVE

BUILD THE PRACTICE UP, HAVE AN ASSOCIATE RUN THE CLINICAL ASPECT AND STILL OWN IT AND MANAGE IT AS AN ABSENTEE OWNER

If you still enjoy the capacity to own your own practice and aren't ready to fully retire or sell your practice, you can consider building it up and bringing in an Associate. This type of associate would be one who can essentially run the day-to-day aspects of the practice and handle all the clinical aspects, but doesn't necessarily own a practice quite yet. You would still have your name on the practice, but would become an absentee owner. If you have created excellent systems and have trained your staff well, a reasonably compete associate should be able to run the practice, as long as they don't get in the way of the system. If they can listen to patients and demonstrate good communication skills, they could have an excellent experience growing into the role of owning the practice.

Many experienced dentists get tired of running a business and would love the opportunity to simply "do the dentistry". If they have done all the legwork necessary to create the business, train the staff, and market the business, many doctors would be happy to just step in and do the dentistry in the private practice model.

As a senior "semi-retired" dentist, you may enjoy stepping in periodically for the younger dentist when they need vacation coverage or when they are away at a seminar. This allows you to keep your "fingers wet" and monitor the pulse of your practice. It also helps give you an opportunity to still have control over the business in case you need to step back into the practice if something happens to the associate.

By hiring a dentist to handle the day-to-day clinical aspect of your practice, you perpetuate the *earning potential machine* you created, allowing you active income, but also "keeping the principal". Most likely, it will provide you a higher rate of return holding onto the practice, than if you sold it and either let that money sit in the bank or put it in some risky investment.

If you are able to stretch out your actual "full retirement" (which means not selling your practice quite yet,) using this model, you could delay dipping into your social security benefits, while at the same time having fewer years you would need for your savings to last you over your lifetime – thereby stretching your retirement savings out longer. The key would be to make sure the associate keeps up the value of the practice (maintains production levels) and not let it plateau or go down. The loss in value that would result from a decrease in the value of the practice could outweigh the marginal income you could earn by having an associate run the practice for a few years. This option would work well in case of a temporary long-term disability or family emergency that causes a doctor to need to step out of the practice earlier than anticipated.

As with any associate arrangement, you should make what is expected and what can and cannot be done as a dentist in your practice clear. Many of these topics have been brought up already, but issues such whether if you will pay for their continuing education? If they can work on their family at a discounted rate—and how far out the term "family" covers – dependents and parents or does it include aunts and uncles and cousins, etc.?

There is also the question of liability. So if you are incorporated, it offers your family some level of protection, however, it might be best to discuss this with your tax attorney.

Finally, you should have the discussion early on, preferably at the same time that you are signing the employment contract, so that if something happens to either one of you, there is a protocol in place to handle the sale of the business properly and equitably.

SECTION FOUR

RETIREMENT TRANSITION STRATEGIES

CHAPTER THIRTEEN

SELLING YOUR PRACTICE TO ANOTHER DENTIST AND CONTINUING TO WORK THERE AS AN ASSOCIATE AT THE PRACTICE

This strategy will only work if the incoming dentist is experienced and can work as fast and efficiently as you did and your practice was growing at a pace to support two dentists. In general, the incoming dentist might expect to earn an income similar to that of the outgoing dentist. However, in reality, not only will there be the added debt due to the loan on buying the practice, but also, they would be sharing that remaining patients (and associated revenue) with the selling dentist. There will most likely be patients who choose to stay with the retiring dentist after the sale because they have a long-term relationship with them and have established trust. As a result, the practice must be in a period of abundance and have great marketing and new patient experiences systems in place to continue. If a practice is in survival mode with a *semi-exiting* dentist, there is little opportunity for a new dentist to share any revenue.

There are THREE primary things that should be evaluated during the transition to make it work: One – you should maximize the capacity of the facility by adding hours, for example, adding evenings and/or weekend appointments to help grow the practice. Secondly, by adding some additional services – if for example, the incoming dentist was offering implants, endo, oral surgery or sedation but referred all those out. Otherwise, if nothing were to change, there would be a smaller piece of the pie for each doctor to split. Finally, you would have to embark on a major marketing effort to increase the practice in order to get enough patients to keep both doctor's schedules full.

The new owner now has the right to change the staff, the fee schedule, adjust YOUR schedule and decide how to split up any new patients. In addition, they may have a difference of opinion on how to treat patients moving forward. The new dentist could be more conservative or more aggressive in their treatment diagnosing. Both of these options could potentially cause a significant shift as regards the productivity of the office. If you sell your practice but continue to work there, you will need to accept the fact that you don't own the practice anymore. If the new dentist sells your fish tank, remodels the office, or fires a long-term employee, you will have no say in it.

If the selling dentist just didn't want to manage the practice but still needs to work for a living, there could be a concern from the purchasing dentist about "giving" all the prime patients who need a lot of work to the selling dentist to keep him happy, while at the same time, handling all the procedures the selling dentist said he doesn't want to handle anymore. After a few months, when the reality of the practice debt sets in, the new dentist will want to "keep" some of the more profitable procedures in their own schedule. It is not unreasonable to think that many of the long-term loyal patients will want to stay with the seller dentist and not "switch-over" to the newer dentist. This could become a problem if it is not discussed in advance.

It is reasonable to be of the opinion that if you split it out on paper that it could potentially work. However, considered from the perspective of transitioning from being an owner to becoming an employee, there is an emotional component to it that might make the work less satisfying. In addition, once all "your" patients who wanted to see you complete their treatment are finished, unless you are continuing to market for yourself, your loyal patient-base will start to dwindle, since you are no longer the owner of the practice. The procedures you are responsible for may turn out to be simply re-treating any broken or fractured teeth on your own patients, and it would become slowly less and less profitable or fulfilling for you. It would entail a slow phasing out of the dental office with no simple solution to it at this point. You probably would have signed a covenant to not compete when you sold the practice so you can't even help out local dental colleagues in the area with their complicated cases or during vacation or medical leave coverage.

This can become a risky gamble if you wish to do it for more than one year, unless you both acknowledge that you will need to expand the marketing and continue to grow the business. Remember that once you sell your practice, you no longer own it and it could cost more than a few hundred thousand dollars in potential retirement income if the deal goes sour. If the practice begins to struggle financially, you will not own your practice, nor have your retirement dream job, nor have a simple option to recreate it without a significant effort. If business drops off, the new owner may look to letting you go first, to save the work for themselves, and you would have little say in that decision.

Another option exists, of selling your practice in such a way that it has a better chance of providing an ongoing retirement transition for you. By finding a dentist who has a similar size practice but wishes to ambitiously expand their business with management and ownership responsibilities included, you could sell them your practice. Instead of asking for the entire price of the practice up front, you could only ask for perhaps a 20 - 25% initial investment. Then, if you wished to work for another 5 - 8 years, they could spread the balance over that length of time, while you back down your schedule from 4 - 5 days a week to only 2 - 3 days a week. You focus on those procedures you enjoy, the long-term patients you have bonded with, and refer the new dentist the rest of the work. When you take your income from working 2 - 3 days a week and add the money from the installments for the practice purchase (plus interest) you should be able to take home the same amount of money each month, or possibly even more, depending upon how long you structure your transitioning! You would gain all this without the headache of running a business, plus you would be having 4 - 5 days off each week! In addition, if the facilities were a little smaller and you wished to do an occasional Saturday or evening shift, you could feasibly alternate your schedules each week and have between 2 - 8 days off every two weeks!

If for whatever reason, you feel that you need to cut back your hours due to issues relating to stamina, health or a progressive illness or condition, an earlier sale of your practice handles the typical situation of having to let your practice decline as your health falters, then running into the challenge of selling your diminished practice at a lower fee. Taking it to the extreme, if you were to die or suffer a critical injury, without having a transition program already in place, your family might need to step up and attempt to scramble together a sale. Typically, when that happens, the value of the practice plummets quickly and your estate will take a serious loss.

Undertaking an early "sale" and *a 5 – 8 year* phase-out transition offers the incoming dentist buying the practice (or merging theirs with yours) a much easier financing option, since both business are already producing income. If they approached a bank with these variables, they would be much more likely to receive 100% financing on their request. Again, depending upon the length of the phase-out, the selling doctor would have received interest which is higher than the banks would have paid typically and would still be able to practice.

One of the intangible assets of a practice is the *"goodwill"* of that practice. So, if the current doctor stays with the practice, the current relationship between the doctor and the patients are maintained. This is potentially a huge benefit to the new doctor as it carries over for another 5 - 8 years, while they pick up speed and also get to know many of those patients. The patients will maintain a loyalty to the practice and still feel a continuity in the care this way.

The advantage to the purchasing dentist is that they also get many of the benefits of a partnership, or a group practice, without many of the accompanying challenges. Some of these include the potential for shared emergency coverage after hours, camaraderie, lower fixed overhead to production ratio and other shared expenses that only larger practices or groups take advantage of.

Again, a well-written contract by an experienced team of attorneys and practice sales brokers, between the buyer and the seller can potentially revert many unforeseen issues in the future. It may cost a little more upfront, but save thousands of dollars later on.

SECTION FOUR

RETIREMENT TRANSITION STRATEGIES

CHAPTER FOURTEEN

SELLING YOUR PRACTICE AND RETIRING FROM DENTISTRY:

According to a study conducted by the Rand Corp. in 2017, authored by Nicole Maestas, 40% of the people who retire end up going back to work in the same or a similar type position. This could be due to boredom, or financial reasons. It is important to have done your homework with a financial planner before taking the step to exit the workplace. If there is a way for older dentists to maintain the feeling of making a difference in people's lives in a meaningful career, with more flexibility in their work hours, many dentists would probably stay longer in the profession longer.

Many people think that selling their dental practice will allow them a lengthy period of financial freedom, or settle their money as regards the income from the sale of the practice. The truth is that the money you receive (assuming that it is a lump sum) is just like winning the lottery (only smaller). After paying the transitions broker, paying off any residual office debt, paying a large chunk in taxes, paying off any outstanding credit card debt or personal loans, putting away some money towards balancing your home mortgage or taking a well-deserved vacation, there probably will be significantly lesser money left than you might have hoped. Most dentists find that after about 18 months, they are starting to rely on other savings to pay their bills. Most likely, you will be spending more on daily living carrying out activities, or pursuing your hobbies, or traveling, or spoiling your grandchildren, so your actual monthly personal spending might go up.

You may want to hire a Practice Broker to help guide you through the sale of your practice. An experienced broker will be able to compare similar practices and give you an idea of what the market is like and how much you could expect from the sale. They can also help you find a buyer and make sure that both parties are doing their due diligence at the beginning of the transaction. They want the sale to be successful, so they will make sure that the buyer is qualified, the value of the practice remains, and the process goes through without a hitch.

FROM THE BUYER'S PERSPECTIVE:

Typically, the goal would be to attempt to retain as many of the patients in the practice as possible for as long as possible. These are the patients that helped to create the value of the practice and contributed to the monthly income that the practice produced. As a buyer, there are certain steps that if taken and followed through, can minimize attrition. In general, since patients know that they will be needing to find a new dentist anyways; when the seller retires or leaves the practice, they might as well give the new buyer a shot at keeping them. The patients know the staff, the location, and the office, and have their history of treatment, so there are advantages to continuity in care, if they stay. It is expected that an additional 10 - 15% of the practice patient base will be lost right off because of personal or distance concerns. The patients who stay with the practice and travel a distance to follow the previous dentist after *they* move out of the area are going to be the tougher ones to hold onto. They may stay with the practice if they had a history with the dentist, and completed a complicated or involved series of treatments that they hope the new dentist will be able to finish or maintain, such as orthodontics or dental implants. They may also stay because the office offered some "niche" service that they trusted and would be willing to have the opportunity to continue with, such as sedation dentistry, TMJ therapy, or holistic dentistry.

If the new dentist changes things up too quickly to customize the practice to their personal likings, for example, by undertaking a major remodel, moving the practice down the street, or switching out a significant number of key employees, patients may feel that they either won't get the same care they were used to, or may not hold that same "loyalty" to the office.

From the buyer's perspective, they should make sure to include as a condition of purchase, that the lease can be successfully transferred to the new buyer, along with an option to renew. The last thing you want is to go through all the financing issues and terms and then find out at the last minute that the landlord intends to sell the building soon, or even kick out the tenants and rent the space to their nephew instead! In addition, you need to find out the future plans of the landlord and have an attorney review the lease to make sure that they don't restrict you from your plans to be open on evenings and weekends in order to expand the practice. It might be a good time to handle this when discussing with the landlord about any changes or additions or other renovations that you have been considering for the practice.

The buyer should also get their own representative or agent to review everything. If the seller has an agent, they will be looking after the seller's best interests. Do not be talked into using the same agent. They will be doing everything they can to make the sale because it takes a lot of time to find and ramp up another buyer typically. You should also have your attorney review all the contracts, and your accountant double check all the income and expense sheets to make sure everything looks in order. Ideally, both these individuals will have good previous experience in the dental field.

When you want to purchase a home, you become a more desirable prospective buyer if you are pre-qualified by the banks. Unfortunately, with dental practices, it doesn't work the same way. They won't tell you that you qualify for a certain amount. They base the loan on a number of factors, most of them related to your experience, your debt load, and the appraised value of the dental practice. While it is not a bad idea to discuss with your bank and have your last few tax returns ready for the time it is needed to prove credibility, they won't give you a number, not so much as even a guideline as to what you should probably be looking for. Once they get numbers from the practice broker, they forge ahead to letting you know (using their own formulas), your lending limit. Often, they will like it if you can put some of your own money into the deal as it proves commitment.

FROM THE SELLER'S PERSPECTIVE:

A larger percentage of new graduates coming out of dental school are almost "forced" in going into a group practice or the corporate scenario, as a result of which the number of potential buyers for a sole proprietorship practice lessening. This is due to the increasing amount of dental school debts causing the banks to be more cautious about loaning money to persons who has never run a business before, and with a massive debt to begin with. As mentioned earlier, less than 15% of the students graduate with no debt, with the average debt exceeding $250,000. As a result, the values of independent dental practices are starting to go down. The balance between working all the time to cover their debt plus a potentially additional practice loan while attempting to have a life outside of the practice is daunting.

Corporate dentistry is finding that sometimes it is easier to simply expand their reach and market heavier, rather than purchasing smaller solo dental practices and converting them or merging them into their model. As a result, the practices that will survive must incorporate some type of "niche" dentistry that corporate doesn't wish to go after. The current trends we have discussed earlier include TMJ, sleep dentistry or aiming for the elderly patients who often prefer a stronger relationship with their dentist and often don't have insurance to dictate where they go for care. So, if you are considering selling your practice within 3 - 5 years, you may wish to focus more energy on developing more of a specialty or niche practice.

If you are selling your practice outright, you may not want the staff to know until the very end when everything is ready to go. On the other hand, if you are staying (as an associate), it is typically a good idea to introduce the seller to the staff prior to the transition and get the staff to "buy into" the transition as well. If they know that you are transitioning and are willing to help, they can even give input on potential buyers. Since the staff understand that this change will affect their own situation and jobs at the office, it can be helpful if they understand and are "on board" with the change. In some cases, it will be good to present the "change" to the staff all at once. If you have a loyal, long-term employee, they might appreciate a small advance notice before you tell the rest of the team so they can get used to the idea and help the others accept the change.

Typically, the new dentist will often be allowed to use the selling dentist's name, often for a period of one year – on their stationery, the building, and when answering the telephone to help give a feel of continuity to the patients. During the upcoming months, the new buyer will be busy transferring the electric bill, the phone bill, the dental supply and lab bills, the lease for the building, any equipment warranties, licenses, registrations, etc. to their name. Many of these are simple, but some of them require the seller to sign a release of control or ownership, so it is handy if the selling dentist stays local or available to help with the transition in those cases. Some of these minor transitional forms can take hours to transfer or get through to the proper authorities and get approved.

In addition, in some cases, there may be several patients who will be upset with the change, and if the selling dentist can comfort them, it will help with the transition. As many people know, when it has to do with *personal space* such as with hair stylists or dentists, many people don't like to change easily. Typically, the seller dentist will have to prepare a letter of appreciation for the patients thanking them for their loyalty along with an introduction of the new dentist and their "blessings", for the transition to go on smoothly, since you have done all that is necessary to make sure that they are well taken care of.

Both the buyer and the seller should be doing their *"due-diligence"* on each other in terms of background, quality of care, practice style, references, etc. to ensure a smooth transfer. This would be especially important if the selling dentist wishes to either finance part of the loan or continue as an associate for a determined period of time to help with rounding up cases and aiding in the transition of the patients.

Once you have found someone who is interested in purchasing your practice, it is prudent to have them sign a LETTER OF INTENT before you can take the practice off the market or start sharing confidential details about your practice. The LOI should be prepared after the buyer has done their initial evaluation and you have done your evaluation of their skills and personality and ability to handle the business. At this point, if not sooner, a BROKER should be involved in the discussions. It basically prohibits both the potential buyer as well as the seller from changing their minds or changing the agreement details. While it may not be a legal binding contract, it is viewed as a professional agreement, and is frowned upon if you change your mind. If you have a few potential buyers interested in your practice, it is good. Take your time to choose your successor. If someone comes in and starts criticizing everything or trying to say they wouldn't be able to duplicate your kind of numbers or that your niche is too specific and that they want to offer you something significantly less that you are looking for, perhaps they are NOT the right person for that practice. It's like buying a car. If it doesn't fit your needs or lifestyle, you can feel it. Talk to the next person and be patient, the right buyer will come along. Plus, you don't want to be sharing all your marketing ideas and practice stats only to find that they changed their mind and opened an office down the street.

It's best to wait on discussing the terms of the sale until you have agreed upon the timing and the price. You may be offering them something they don't need or want (i.e. financing or payment options). While it would be prudent to discuss your options with a competent tax person, in general, it could be safer and less complicated to receive the full purchase price up front. This is especially true if you do not plan on going back into practice. There may be situations in which you might consider taking part payments – for example, if your child was taking over the practice, then you could stretch out the payments to make it affordable for them and use the money as part of your retirement. You may also consider taking partial payment if you hired a younger associate, later in your career and you trust them fully and feel confident that they could do well with the practice—meaning catch up to the production levels you were achieving or even exceed them by adding more services. The last thing you want is a buyer defaulting on their loan, requiring you to dust off your clinical jacket and go back to practice once you have retired, just to maintain the value of the business until you resell it again (depending upon the way the arrangement is set-up.)

It might be challenging to you to step back into the practice after a year or two and trying to pick up where you left off. If the loan is fully paid off, then what happens to the practice is no longer your concern from a financial perspective.

There are tax advantages to you selling off the practice over time, however, your accountant is in the best position to advice you on that.

Finally, if you have a comprehensive retirement plan set up and don't need to work anymore, the additional income from a phased payment plan is always nice. Most likely, you would be taxed at a lower rate in a phased payment plan.

HOW TO SELECT A PRACTICE BROKER:

When you have made the decision to sell your practice, the next step is to select the best practice broker to help you through the process. How do you determine which one will take the best care of you and assist you in getting the most for your practice? There are many brokers out there and choosing the best one for you is like selecting a real estate agent. You should look at references, check Online reviews, ask colleagues, check with your local dental society and do your homework.

Just as with real estate sales, you could have one broker represent both the buyer and the seller or you could each have a representative watching out for your individual needs. A buyer should put together their own team independently, to properly evaluate the practice before signing any Letter of Intent with the seller. If for whatever reason your practice is appraised at a lower value than you were expecting (which is common), it is OK to ask for the reasons, or discuss the reasons you believe that your practice should be worth higher. It is always a good idea to discuss this *before* you submit an amount to a potential buyer. If there was a shift in the local economy, you suffered a temporary disability, took a long vacation, or were having staff changes that contributed to a down year, you can explain that. If there were significant additions and growth in the practice one year ago that isn't represented in the prior years, you can explain that and see if they will stand behind a higher value.

The broker you select can help you in many ways. They can help you prepare your practice and suggest items that might increase the appeal of your practice, they can help you evaluate it and appraise it for you, they can help you find a buyer, and much more. In the end though, you should have a competent small business tax attorney review all the documents before you sign or share anything with the potential buyer.

An experienced broker will not commit to the value of a practice until they have looked at your last three years income and expense sheets, the age of your equipment, the location of your office, the overall overhead and the number of dental benefit plans you are involved with. Part of the value of an experienced broker is that they see that the superficial numbers an office presents may or may not represent the true story of the practice.

If the practice broker finds a potential buyer, the broker should without fail have them sign a Non-Disclosure Agreement before they get any details about the practice. This will help protect confidential information about the practice, and the fact that it is for sale. The last thing you want is your staff and your community finding out that you are retiring.

DETERMINING THE VALUE OF A DENTAL PRACTICE:

There are several methods for determining the value of a dental practice. Some typical factors are location, the number of active patients, the age of the practice, the longevity and quality of the current staff, how old the equipment is, if the patients in the practice are mostly fee-for-service or if you have a lot of reduced fee dental plans in your practice, if the practice is growing or shrinking, if the practice has shown consistent growth over the last few years and how profitable the practice is. Some of the less obvious factors would include: The mix of procedures done in the practice, any area of dentistry the current dentist specializes in (if they handle a lot of certain procedures such as implants, sedation or TMJ), what some of the major sources of new patients are, the skills of the selling dentist in terms of leadership of the practice, selling dentistry, and the speed and quality of the care provided. Obviously, if the new dentist prefers to take two hours to prepare a crown and make a temporary crown but the selling dentist only needed 15 minutes and used to have his staff make the temporary crown, then the practice styles of the two dentists must be taken into consideration.

While it might be exciting and seem fun for two dental school friends fresh out of school to buy a busy practice and try to split it up, there is a risk as regards them being able to keep up the same level of production without doubling the overhead by having two dentists wanting an income along with the debt from the purchase of the practice. Therefore, it is always good to have a trained practice transitions specialist run a few scenarios for you on paper and include a slightly higher than average attrition along with adding debt to see if there still is room for profitability. It is anticipated that the first year of a practice will be tougher as you are figuring out all the materials, equipment, getting to know the business systems, staff, as well as the patients.

To an experienced dentist who already has their speed up and systems in place, a busy practice will have more potential value than to a newer dentist. In general, if the personalities of the two dentists (buyer and seller) are similar and their practice styles and philosophies are similar, it would bode a much higher degree of success for the transition. If the selling dentist is well known in the community, church, or with local sports or charitable organizations, the purchasing dentist might have a tougher time filling those shoes. Because these activities and personalities of a practice evolve over time, it may not seem as obvious to a selling dentist that it should be difficult for a buying dentist to simply jump in and "take over" as they exit the practice.

A competent practice broker will put all the numerical information they gather and add in the modifiers that affect the practice growth in the future and look at debt, equipment, staff and the array of procedures and give a value based upon the supply of potential candidates out there. Other factors such as accounts receivables can modify the value up or down as well. Most buyers prefer not to purchase the accounts receivables, so it is best as you get closer to the sale, to attempt to clear up this number to as low as possible. The reason they might *want* to purchase the A/R is because they will do so at a reduced amount based upon the aging of the accounts, and it offers opportunity for passive income.

There are three traditional evaluation methods that brokers will discuss with their clients when coming up with a value, and often they will take these three methods and take the average. A simple explanation of the three methods is given here:

There is the **ASSET APPROACH** which focuses more on the age and quality of the equipment, facilities, furniture, instruments, supplies, etc. and assigning a current market value to each item, then adding in the goodwill of the practice. This part is more important for tax purposes. It can be a little frustrating to the owner when they find that an equipment they purchased only a couple years ago has an asset value of 20 - 30% of what they paid for it. There is a little room for discussion but not much. The *GOODWILL* of the practice is often calculated roughly at around 40% of the last year's annual gross revenues. There are a number of factors that are looked at when actually calculating the goodwill of the practice. (Reputation, ratio of private paying clients to those with dental network coverage, staff, location, source of new patients, rural or urban, client demographics, etc.)

There is the **INCOME APPROACH** which focuses on the future potential income accruable to the buyer, based upon earnings history. It looks at what the buyer can afford to pay for the practice. It is almost like a big brother looking out for the buyer to let them know if the numbers will work for them as a buyer. They include a risk assessment for the practice and factor inflation in order to develop a spreadsheet for predicting when the new buyer can realistically anticipate a good return. They want to make sure that the purchaser can get their investment back in approximately four years. (This is sometimes referred to as determining the *Capitalization Rate*. The dentistry standard is a 25 percent capitalization rate, although depending upon a variety of factors it could be between 20 - 25%)

Then there is the **MARKET COMPARISON APPROACH** which looks at what the similar practices in the area have sold for and compares the specifics of the office and raises or lowers the value based upon values applied to each item (i.e. age of equipment, location, Fee-For-Service, PPO's, Medicaid ratio, reputation, etc.). This calculation starts with the Gross Collections of the practice and develops a ratio for comparing it to other practices selling for around that same price.

Going into the specific details and value of each approach is beyond the scope of this book. Just remember that high production numbers don't always mean a high net income. Therefore, it is prudent to look at those ratios when comparing. The practice broker will most likely want to study the last few years tax returns to see the true earnings potential of the practice.

Despite the need to do a comprehensive evaluation before quoting a price, according to Stanley Pollock, BS, DMD, MS, PhD, JD, MCBA, MCMEA, ABAR in his book ***BVR's GUIDE TO VALUING DENTAL PRACTICES***, the dental practices that were sold in the 1980's often closed for 100% of the last 12 months gross revenues. During the next 20 years prices actually went up a little higher, but then came down to only *65% of the previous year's collected revenues* on average. Remember, your practice is not average! Every practice is unique and has their own set of great things going for it as well as challenges. Therefore, if you have time to get your practice "ready" to sell, you may be able to effectively address and get your numbers in alignment for the best valuation possible.

In 2008, the ADA did a survey of new dentists purchasing practices. They found that the average amount spent in the U.S. to buy into a partnership, start from scratch, or practice ranged from $457,600 - $472,390. Dentists who purchased an ongoing practice, versus someone starting from scratch had the advantage of an ongoing system in place, with staff already familiar with the day-to-day operations and an existing patient base for only an additional $20,000 (a great deal if all other things are equal!). The current patients if taken care of well, can be potential source of new patients, as well from referrals. Having a working system adds a lot of value to an existing practice.

One final note on appraisals. If you are a specialty practice and have a buyer who is brand new to your practice or to the area, the transferable value of the practice you bought is not the same as that of a general practice. Typically, a relationship would exist between you and the referring dentists rather than the patient base. With the exception of orthodontics, most patients will make three or fewer visits to that specific specialist, so the value of the patient base is not as important as the reputation of the practice in the community. If you are able to transition the practice to an associate over time, they will typically get more value for the sale of the practice.

HOW DO YOU QUANTIFY THE "GOODWILL" OF A PRACTICE?

The GOODWILL of a dental practice is considered an "intangible" asset. In other words, Goodwill is calculated partly using factual data, such as the number of active patient charts, history of progressive sustainable growth over the past few years, and demographics of the customer or patient base. It also has a few components that could be more subjectively valued, such as the doctor's reputation in the community, realistic expectations of earnings, practice debt, realistic evaluation of overhead ratios in the past, and the mix of services provided by the office. Other considerations include: if the practice is held as a corporation, if there are supplemental benefits given to the doctor or their family, and if the lease is easily transferable and the facilities are intact.

The Buyer of the practice will most likely want to allocate as much of the practice price to the practice assets since those can can be depreciated quickly, whereas items like goodwill and other intangible assets need to be depreciated over periods of up to 15 years. The complete tax ramifications depend on whether the business is a sole proprietorship, a partnership, or an LLC, are beyond the scope of this book. Since the rules are continually changing, it is always a good idea to involve a tax specialist, an attorney, and a practice broker in the purchase or sale of any business. Whether the income from the sale of the practice is taxed as capital gains, inside a corporate tax structure, or as "ordinary income" will determine your tax basis. The allocation of the components of the sale, such as tangible assets like equipment and supplies vs. the intangible assets such as goodwill and Covenant Not to Compete will also have different tax consequences to both the buyer and the seller. This is all part of the conversations you should be having with your broker when you come up with a price for the practice.

GETTING YOUR PRACTICE "READY" TO SELL.

Once you have decided that you want to sell your practice in the near future, it is prudent to contemplate not only from the buyer's perspective, but also from the bank or lender's perspective what would make a practice more desirable. Practice transition strategies are best planned out between five to ten years in advance to allow you time to line up coaches, your practice numbers, your attorneys, accountants, and practice brokers, so that when that right time comes, you and your numbers will shine.

NET INCOME. Obviously, a practice that has a low overhead and high margin of profit will have a higher valuation and be more desirable to someone wishing to buy as well as to a bank lending the money for the business. Some banks often use this guideline – 5.5 times the net income of a business is the maximum they loan out. If there is real estate associated with the practice, that is added into the equation and they would allow more in the loan. Most banks will also want to see the last 3 years' Profit and Loss Statements with explanations of any large purchase documents as well as any other non-recurring expenses.

NEW EQUIPMENT. If your practice has recently purchased new equipment, a lender is going to want to make sure that any outstanding loans are paid off prior to the sale. Essentially all large existing debt associated with a business would ideally have to be paid off before the banks will give a loan to a new buyer. Unfortunately, when you purchase new equipment in the last year or two of practicing before you sell, you will not get a good return on your investment from resale value. Nonetheless, if the purchase of new equipment increases your ability to potentially provide more dentistry (CAD/CAM crown machine, updated computer system, 3D Cone Beam or Hard Tissue Laser, for example,) and makes the practice more attractive to a new buyer, then you could break-even on the investment. You might be lucky to get a value of 20-30% of a purchase price on small to mid-sized equipment purchases made in the last couple of years.

TIMING. Sometimes you might enjoy handling the dentistry, but find that you need to cut back because of the mental drain or your physical ability to handle the same full schedule you did years ago. If you begin to cut back your days or your hours, you are lowering the potential value of your practice. A broker will look at the last three years' collections when determining the value of your practice and if they see a serious declining trend from three consecutive "down" years, this could cost you hundreds of thousands of dollars when you go to sell. Therefore, when you begin to consider serious retirement, the time to start planning is probably five years in advance to best set-up your practice for transition.

QUALITY OF PATIENTS. If you are in a high-volume practice that accepts every dental plan out there, it might be time to consider focusing on attracting the "right" type of patients that will make your practice more desirable to a potential buyer. By focusing on building quality relationships with fewer patients that desire a higher quality of care and are willing to pay extra for it. Around 25% of the people out there are willing to pay a little more for comfort, relationship, and comprehensive care. It is your job to build a practice that attracts that type of patient.

FACILITIES. Just as selling a house that is freshly painted might be more desirable to more people; a clean, modern office will also bring in a higher dollar when you are ready to sell. If you have exotic tastes or decorations in your office unrelated to dentistry, you may consider "toning it down" a bit to make it more conventional but still professional. New carpeting, new paint, or some new furniture can give an older office a quick "facelift" and at the same time, update the office. If the building space next door has the capacity to offer you more room to expand into their space, that can be a bonus. A new buyer might have bigger ambitions to bring in other dentists or specialists into the practice. You should discuss the transition with your landlord if you made a lease to make sure that they will be accommodating to the new owner or growth plans.

CLEAN UP YOUR PRACTICE MANAGEMENT DATABASE. With most offices being computerized these days, it is very easy to generate reports. You could generate a report of all outstanding accounts over 90 days, a report of patients with no appointments in the last year (and nothing scheduled currently), and all patients with unscheduled treatment plans. In addition, if your practice is one that has a lot of pre-payments, you may want to attempt to finish up the work that was paid for, so that when the transition occurs, any credits on the accounts will be minimal. In addition, you should take a realistic look at patients that haven't had an appointment within the last 24 months, and unless they are on an extended vacation, you should probably consider them "inactive". In some rural areas, that figure might be extended to 36 months due to accessibility, with "active" patients inclusive. With most practice management systems, this will still keep their data in the computer, but they won't receive patient statements, or be counted as active patients when considering the value of the practice. If you have patients who have had balances outstanding for over two years without any payments, you need to seriously consider writing them off, as a dental insurance plan will not be paying anything at this point, and it is obvious (unless they are relatives or close friends) that they have no intention of paying or even think that they owe the office anything. If they have a large balance and continually make promises and either don't follow-up on their promises or dribble in a very small amount that wouldn't even cover the interest, it might be a nice gesture to offer a significant *discount to pay* and take care of the balance with a credit card over the phone right then. Otherwise you will be receiving pennies on the dollar for long outstanding account balances of inactive patients. Another thing to do is to clean up duplicate insurance plan entries and duplicate Employer Names. Often, these might get entered by two different people and then you start two different lists. If you can delete and transfer one of the lists to the other employer or plan, it will make updating benefits significantly easier for the new dentist.

MARKET AND DEMOGRAPHIC RESEARCH. If you can show that large influx of people come into your geographic area often, or that a large new business will bring in a potential flood of patients in the future, that could increase the potential of your practice. If you get a significant portion of your new patients from referrals versus having to spend thousands of dollars on local area marketing, it might make the practice more desirable. Avoid any major changes in your marketing strategies close to the timing of your sale. You don't want to show a drop-off of new patients or a marked increase, because it will not significantly help with the prior 2 - 3 year's accounting numbers, which is what will be analyzed. Nor will it look good if you have a drop in new patients or production occurring just before a sale.

STABILITY OF YOUR TEAM. You can't always control how long your staff have been with you at the time of your sale. However, if your staff have been with you for years, it demonstrates a more stable practice to a potential buyer than if your staff have been there an average of less than one year. Having a solid employee manual with policies and procedures in place is helpful to keeping staff on track. A new dentist may bring in their own manual and change everything or they may adopt your policies if things are smooth flowing in the practice. Avoid giving raises or making promises of employment if there will be a new owner. In some areas, the new owner is required to continue to keep the current office staff in their employment for a specific time, otherwise they could be held accountable for labor board issues or possibly fines. Fortunately, the majority of the time, staff would rather stay at a practice that they are familiar with the patients, familiar with the other staff, and already know how to operate all the equipment. They just don't know the new doctor or his mannerisms or practice style. They would have to learn that at a different office anyways, so they generally will give the new dentist a chance, just like the patients will. They assume that the owner-dentist has done their due diligence and researched the new dentist to make sure in advance that they would be a good "fit" for the office. Since they trusted the prior owner, they would trust his choice of successors as well.

MIX OF SERVICES OFFERED. If sedation and dental implants make up 80% of your income, then it might be considered a "niche" practice. This means that a potential buyer might look at it and not be interested if they didn't already do dental implants or sedation. Your patients have grown to expect that and while it is a great way to build a practice, there are a very narrow group of dentists that could thrive in that environment. Other examples of "niche" practices are ones that specialize in cosmetic veneers, sleep disorder dentistry, holistic dentistry, or TMJ dentistry. While these practices are unique and great to specialize in, when it's time to sell, they are potentially less desirable to the bulk of new dentists looking for a practice. From the perspective of a new dentists, they would love a practice where the previous owner referred out all the pediatric dentistry, root canals, extractions, implants, and TMJ treatment. That type of practice has a lot of built-in potential for internal growth.

MODERNIZE YOUR PRACTICE PRESENCE. If you don't have a website or an updated website, it would be helpful to get your business updated to have the maximum amount of visibility on the web in order to attract patients, as well as have some social media presence. While this may not have been as important ten years ago, this is the arena that most practices are competing in, especially for the growing *millennial* generation. Your facilities should also represent the level of care you provide. Look around the interior and exterior of your office and make sure that it looks current and modern.

THE LOCAL NEIGHBORHOOD. If your practice is located in a very expensive neighborhood, or even a highly impacted commercial business area, it might attract different types of clients as well as buyers. Be prepared to address any potential concerns and keep lists of local dental labs, specialists, and other potential referral sources to make the vision of the practice more realistic and attractive.

TERMS OF THE SALE. As stated earlier, you should wait to discuss the terms of the sale with your potential buyer until you have a strong commitment from them including a **Letter of Intent**. The letter of intent is basically a non-binding agreement that outlines the basics of your agreement discussed, declaring their interest in buying the practice. You don't want to be throwing out ideas on creative financing just to make the deal work. If you decide to do any type of payment plan, most consultants would suggest not extending it out more than 5 - 7 years at the maximum, if at all. Again, depending on whether you plan on staying with the practice during that *transition pay period* or not would influence whether you should even consider any type of installment. If you stretch out the payments, then the price should go up to make up for the loss of use of that capital if they had paid you in full. Not to mention that the risk of default on the loan is higher the longer it is stretched out.

YOUR BRANDING. If your business name is your personal name, and you have been considering selling within ten years, it might make sense to consider creating a new business entity that can be transferred more easily. The company name will stay with the practice this way and you won't have to worry about changing the name of the practice to the buying dentist's name.

MAKE SURE YOU HAVE A GOOD ACCOUNTANT. You want to make sure your books look "clean" and easy to understand with any and all expenses itemized properly and properly categorized. A clean set of books that are laid out in QuickBooks spreadsheets or some similar program are going to be more reliable than the handwritten pegboard system that your mom or your sister had been helping you run your practice with for the past 20 years.

THINGS TO LOOK OUT FOR IN A PRACTICE SALES CONTRACT:

When you sign your contract to sell your practice, you want to have as few questions and as many solid game plans to handle any number of circumstances that might come up in the future. As mentioned earlier, as a seller, your goal is to make sure that the buyer dentist is as successful in their venture as they would like to be. While you can share how you ran your practice or encourage them to do certain things, it is now *their* practice to do whatever they want with.

Here are a few guidelines that your contract should cover so that there are no foreseeable misunderstandings:

1. A clear plan on how to handle retreatment or repairs in the event of restoration breaks or when an appliance needs repair. Specify a timeframe that you are willing to either come into the office to handle the repairs or to reimburse the buying dentist (typically at a discounted fee) to take care of the warranty themselves.

2. Establish and agree upon a clear protocol for presenting the retreatment case with photos, or x-rays to justify the need for the repair or replacement, along with the age of the restoration and approximate cost of repair.

3. Select a local trusted colleague that you both can agree on, to refer to in the event that you have a dispute on how to handle retreatment on a case.

4. A specific timeline during which the new dentist can utilize your name associated with the practice marketing or communications going forward. Typically, this should be one year.

5. Unless it is obvious that you are not going to be continuing practicing dentistry, the new dentist will most likely want some type of Covenant Not To Compete or Solicit Clause. The time frame and the distance can be agreed upon based on what type of community you live in, whether it is a high-density population or more rural. This could include solicitation of the staff to go work for another colleague.

6. If you are doing any marketing or have contracts with web page companies or yellow page companies, the time frame or possibility for transferring or cancelling any ongoing contracts should be discussed.

7. You may wish to discuss with the incoming dentist about what supplies they like or don't use, as well as smaller pieces of equipment they might like or won't use. This will help you when ordering supplies and repairing equipment close to the time of the sale so that you don't waste money on stocking up items they will not even want.

8. The same is true with any maintenance companies, computer servicing companies, medical waste pick-ups, equipment warranties, licenses, etc.

9. A discussion should be had with the landlord in advance if you are leasing your office, to make sure that they are not planning on selling the building and are willing to let you pass the lease through them to a new tenant.

10. A detailed list of any or all personal items at the office that the selling dentist may wish to hang on to after the sale. This could be more important if they have a strong theme in the practice related to either the selling dentist's name or their hobbies.

11. Look to see if there are any significant past due accounts receivables. This might be the sign of a practice with poorly run financial arrangements set-up. Or, it could mean that they do a lot of orthodontics and do in-office financing. Either way, during a transition, patients sometimes may change their minds about paying off a new dentist for work started by a previous one. It is always best to attempt to avoid adding new long-term payment plans and clean-up old ones when getting ready to sell.

12. It would be good to have your tax attorney do an assessment of anticipated taxes on the sale of the practice before you sign the paperwork so that you can be prepared once everything is signed.

FINDING A BUYER FOR YOUR DENTAL PRACTICE

There are many avenues that you can take when looking for a buyer. It could come about from conversations with your buddies at the dental society meetings or local study clubs. It might be prudent not to tell your staff about selling until you are closer to the sale as staff may begin to tell patients that you are leaving, especially if the patient was considering embarking on a long-involved series of procedures with the current dentist. They might casually talk the patients out of starting new treatment. In addition, if they had been considering retiring or leaving the practice, this might give them an opportunity to make that move. This could disrupt your longevity of solid staff when selling the practice.

Other avenues for looking for potential buyers include asking the specialists you work with, your supply dealers, equipment sales people, local dental lab people, or specialty niche product sales people (i.e. the local dental implant sales rep.). The dental society may have a classified listing board or the state dental society might have a classified section. In the current market today, there is one young dentist buyer for every four dental practices that are for sale. This means that you might need to investigate the options of finding another practice that may wish to merge their practice with yours, instead of only looking in the new dentist market.

If you are able to bring a potential buyer, it could save you thousands of dollars by not having your broker do the legwork and searching for a match for your practice. When you find the right buyer for your practice, you will know it. They will appreciate the long-term value of your practice and what you have built up, and not try to give you grief every step of the way.

It is OK to decide not to sell your practice to an individual if you do not think that they are a good "fit". After all, you put years of sweat and blood (no pun intended) into building your business and you have a responsibility to your clients to make sure they are taken care of. If you are planning on staying with the practice a while after the transition, you can be a little more lenient as regards some of the criteria that you might have been looking for in the successor to your practice. For example, you might be able to help them learn more about the business, or about a particular aspect of the clinical services you deliver, so that they won't be stuck with a business that they can't handle or sustain. Just as they are doing their research on you and your practice, you should do your due diligence on them as a buyer who will come in with a clean background, no credit blemishes, no Dental Board issues, ability to get Liability Insurance, has a current license in your state, and a DEA license for writing prescriptions.

The other aspect of finding the right buyer is making sure that their communication skills will be up to the level that will sustain your practice. Will they be able to influence patients to accept treatment at the same level that you were able to?

As you get close to thinking about your estate planning and selling, you should be sure that your will, living trust, and durable power of attorney are all in order. The worst thing that could happen is having your family try to decide how to sell your practice or attempt to manage it without your help. Connect with a "Licensed Fiduciary for your Trust" or have a "Letter of Instruction" that guides and lists all your practices' advisors and support people to help them organize the sale in the event of an emergency. This helps to safeguard your practice and your business assets.

If a Dental Management Company approaches you to purchase the practice, make sure that one of the buyers is a dentist who will be working there. The last thing you need is to have them come in, hire and associate to run the business, and pay you over time on a financing schedule. If the practice goes under, the company may default on the loan for any number of reasons they already are prepared for, once they have destroyed and stripped your practice of all the dentistry they can run through it. If it doesn't "feel" right, then hold on for the next offer.

SECTION FIVE

WHAT'S NEXT?

CHAPTER FIFTEEN

- PROTECTING YOUR FUTURE

- ENJOYING YOUR RETIREMENT LIFESTYLE

SECTION FIVE

WHAT'S NEXT?

CHAPTER FIFTEEN

PART ONE: **PROTECTING YOUR FUTURE**

As you prepare to turn over the keys to your practice, there may be a few things that you wish to consider both *prior to completing the sale of your practice* and afterwards, to help make sure that your retirement goes smoothly and that you are prepared.

PERSONAL:

If you have the ability to put away money in a Health Savings Account (HSA). you should consider putting that money away in a tax-deductible account that grows tax-free. The sooner you start doing this, the more you can save up, because *once you retire and enroll in Medicare, you can't contribute anymore*. Healthcare expenses according to Fidelity Investments suggests that even a healthy couple that retire in 2017 will need around an additional $275,000 just to cover their health-related costs in retirement. Even though Medicare will cover some of the out-of-pocket expenses, the cost-sharing portions of the premiums, along with dental expenses, over-the-counter medications and long-term care are not covered. If you need to go into an assisted living situation or a nursing home, those costs can drain a retirement fund rapidly.

The average lifespan of adults has been steadily rising and in fact, the average lifespan of adults back in 1935 when Social Security was enacted was not even 65 years, it was 61.7 years! So, they didn't anticipate having to fund people's retirement for a significant length of time back then if they retired at age 65. Today, the average retirement period is 15 - 20+ years, and with the number of baby boomers entering retirement at a rate higher than ever before, it might make sense to be sure that you fund your own retirement savings well, especially if you are under age 40 years old. It is advised that you go to the Social Security Administration website and secure your own personal Social Security account to prevent someone else from stealing it. When you go there (www.ssa.gov), you can create your own account and update your information to help prevent fraud and ID theft. You can also go there to find out your estimated future Social Security benefits. Since they base your benefits upon your earnings, it's a good idea to keep good records of your earnings. If there is missing information there, it could lower the potential amount of your benefits available.

Once you retire, typically, your source of income is no longer there. If you were fortunate enough to invest in real estate throughout your career, or had a 401k or stocks or bonds set aside to provide an alternate income, congratulations! You should get together with your financial advisors and make sure that you have good short and long-term investment strategies as well as emergency funds set aside.

Diversification of investments is always a good idea. The reason is that it minimizes your anxiety to pull out of one (typically solid) investment if you see trouble. Many of the people who sold their homes or dropped out of the stock market when things went down lost a significant portion of their savings. Often, they pulled them out and shifted into even riskier investments without researching those well. As you get older and closer to retirement, your "risk tolerance" might go down. You would not be able to recover from a downward financial shift easily. When you were younger, if a stock went down 20% you had time on your hands to allow it time, typically up to two years before it reverses its trends, unless it was a true dud. It's always a good idea to meet with *one or more* wealth advisors to get input on what's happening in the market. Poor or outdated advice can cost you hundreds of thousands of dollars. 18 of the top billion-dollar companies that are active today didn't even exist 10 years ago! Only one in eight of the top companies from 50 years ago are even still in business today. The investments that were solid 20 years ago are not the top investments of today. There were years when pulling your money out of the stock market and waiting might have been a good idea, but in the long term, cash sitting in the bank will never outrun inflation.

The ideal goal of a well-structured portfolio is to have one, so that you can live on just the earnings, (meaning the interest and the dividends) and not have to touch the principal. With the economic cycles of recession and recovery, your timing as regards the need to tap into your funds could either be optimal or poor. It is not difficult to predict that the economy will go up and down, it's just difficult to predict exactly *when* it will do that. If housing prices are down when you anticipated selling your home to retire elsewhere, it could mean the loss of hundreds of thousands of dollars. If your assets are diversified, it can offer you the option of delaying cashing out an investment when it is on the low part of the cycle.

When you start spending your savings, and dipping into your retirement plan, and if you have Social Security available as well, there is a systematic approach to spending that will minimize your taxes and maximize your investments. You should consider living off the sale of the practice funds first, since you are taxed on these proceeds anyways. Then you should consider using your Social Security Benefits and personal investments next. This leaves your retirement plan and IRA last, since those are still accumulating tax-deferred income, and will continue to grow. This advice was written up in Dental Economics magazine issue dated July 2011 by John K. McGill, CPD, MBA and Brad Kucharo, CPA, CFP in an article called **Top 10 retirement planning strategies – Part 1**.

Other concerns that you should look into are how you have titled your life insurance policies as well as any real estate properties. While a comprehensive discussion on this would fill numerous books, it is critical that if you wish to leave a legacy to your family, you consider the proper titling of these assets as well. Having a will or a trust that you review every 3 - 5 years, along with a power of attorney for health care and an advance directive are all wise decisions. Iowa State University has put together a comprehensive set of valuable retirement information online that is available for free at: https://www.extension.iastate.edu/humansciences/retirement. While most of the information is universally applicable, there may be tax and property laws that vary by state, so it would be good to get current information from your own state regulations and advisors.

DENTAL PRACTICE:

If you have decided to delay your retirement by working a few more years, whether you decided to sell your practice and work as an associate or go through a long-term installment buy-out, you probably had been able to delay your desire to tap into Social Security. This is one of the best strategies to maximize your S.S. benefits. However, if family or health issues caused you to make changes earlier than anticipated, it's even more important to make sure that your retirement strategies are in order. This includes the timing of the sale of your practice and the timing of you actually quitting practicing dentistry. As discussed earlier in this book, if you will be using the sale your dental practice as part of your retirement strategy, there are several options available to maximize your return on your life's investment.

The time to plan your retirement is not after you retire. Dentists need to design their own custom retirement plan based upon their age, their family, and their profit level. As you get older and as you earn more income, it is even more critical to start solidly planning and evaluating your situation at least every five years. From Simple-IRA's to the more elaborate Tiered Defined Benefit Plans, there is a significant difference in the amounts that you can put away each year. For a mid-career dentist, they may want to look into the workplace retirement type plans that allow employees to start contributing to their own savings plans. By offering them options that include matching funds, this can be an additional benefit for retaining some of your better employees. By adding in eligibility requirements, it will potentially lower your turnover and minimize your costs for including every employee that walks through the door. One draw-back of the more complex plans is that they can get expensive to administer and typically require a Third Party Administrator (TPA). While the TPA will help administer the plan and help you design it, they usually won't offer investment advice, you will still need to consult a tax professional. Each of the various plans have their pluses and minuses. They may either have lower limits or mandatory employee contributions. They could be easy to set up or they can be complex. Some of these programs typically wouldn't work cost-effectively for smaller offices.

One other advantage of putting away money into a qualified retirement savings plan, is that it is protected from lawsuits. For example, as a dentist or other professional, you might be looked at as a good target for a lawsuit. Having your assets protected in a tax-efficient portfolio can be one method of protecting your future. On the other hand, you want to make sure that you don't over-protect your assets such that when you are required to withdraw them you are at a high tax bracket.

Years ago, dentists would consider the sale of their practice as a significant portion of their retirement. Nowadays, with fewer new dentists being able to buy a practice within five years of graduating, and the increase of group practice models, a solo practitioner should begin their transition planning earlier and create alternate options of income during their retirement years. In addition, they need to protect those assets and start as early as possible to watch the trends and stay one step ahead.

As mentioned earlier as well, you will want to make sure that when you do sell your practice, if the new dentist should become injured or not succeed with your practice, depending upon how you structured the sale, it could potentially come back to you. In addition, if the business was misrepresented to the new buyer, that too could trigger potential legal issues. This is why having a solid business structure and good accounting records in your business is critical.

Make sure that you have clearly determined how you will handle retreatments in the practice after the sale, and for how long. If you are able to handle them yourself after you retire, obviously that would be the best option and it would take the least amount of cash out of your pocket.

If you owned your real estate where the practice was, you could collect residual rental income as well as maintain the property and potentially gain appreciation in equity in the building as well. If you do this and can also make the rental agreement a "triple-net" option, then you will not be responsible for maintenance and operating expenses, the renter would pay all that. This allows you the opportunity to enjoy your retirement even more! Another advantage of not selling the real estate with the practice is that it makes the price significantly less for a potential buyer and probably easier to get financing for. Later on, when you decide to sell the property you can ask the new dentist if they are interested, or if you can sell it to any investor.

After you retire, you will want to make sure that you have "tail-end" malpractice insurance coverage. This means that if anything comes up, even after you sell the practice, you will be covered for a certain time period. This is important especially if you handle more involved procedures that have high investments on the part of the patient or a potential to be costly to repair if they don't last as long as the patient might have anticipated it should.

In summary, we highly advise you set up your professional pre-retirement and post-retirement advisory team in advance. This includes:

MEETING WITH YOUR WEALTH MANAGEMENT ADVISOR(S). Just because you are retired doesn't mean you won't need professional coaching anymore. It's time to re-evaluate your current financial needs and future financial needs based upon extended life planning. This would include all kinds of variables including paying for children's life events or grand children's schooling, etc. In addition, it could mean setting up a legacy for your family. They will be able to *guesstimate* how much Social Security will cover during various times in your life, depending upon when you chose to start taking it. They can discuss Medicare options, they can talk to you about the cost of nursing homes, life insurance, and other critical expenses that would be nice to have laid out to avoid surprises later in life. Again, you might consider talking to a few advisors, but don't try to follow 5 - 10 different plans, otherwise, it will get confusing and you will have conflicting investments. Diversify, but in a logical strategic manner. Then meet or keep in touch with your advisors at least annually. Don't blindly let one investment advisor talk you into putting everything into one "sure bet" stock.

REASSESS ALL YOUR INSURANCE PLANS. You most likely will be at a stage where you won't need Disability Insurance and you should look at your investments and your personal life situation to see if your Life Insurance is needed or enough. Make sure that you have updated the beneficiaries in a manner that is consistent with your overall plan. Contact all your Insurance carriers such as Disability Insurance, Business Overhead Insurance and Workers' Compensation, and make sure that they know that you are not in business anymore. If you were over 65 when you begin your final practice transition, you might want to relook at your Disability Coverage options since many of them actually cut-off at a specific age. Therefore, what made sense in the past might not make sense to continue in the future. After age 70, many traditional term life insurance premiums start to go up so high, they may not be worth it anymore or necessary, depending upon your particular estate.

MEET WITH YOUR ATTORNEY. A good business lawyer can help with reviewing your Transition Contract and they can help advise you on how to best protect your assets once you are retired. You may want to also connect up with an Estate Planning Lawyer to make sure you have a Trust, a Living Will, a Healthcare Directive and a Power of Attorney. You should plan on getting together to review these every few years or whenever major life changes occur.

MEET WITH YOUR ACCOUNTANT. Typically, this should be a CPA who can handle all the aspects of the sale of your practice to minimize your taxes and make sure that your practice books are clean and understandable when you are getting them ready for presentation to another dentist. They can also advise you after the sale on how to structure the strategic timing on tapping into your retirement savings to protect and maximize it. You should consider creating a reasonable monthly budget for discretionary spending. (Don't forget to factor in for inflation.) You should also talk about limits on family support so it doesn't become an emotional decision when conditions come up. While paying off your home before you retire is desirable, if it means giving up a significant amount of your liquid assets to do so, it could put you into a bind down the road, if you should need emergency cash or if you have high monthly bills.

TALK WITH OTHER DENTISTS WHO HAVE RETIRED ABOUT RETIREMENT. You will gain valuable insights into what they went through emotionally, and financially after the sale of their practice.

LEAVING A LEGACY. After you retire and quit working, it may be time to think about how you want your assets to be passed on to your heirs. Again, your tax attorney is much more qualified to discuss options, but having a plan to pass assets down over time, may lower tax liability and simplify your estate in the future. By consolidating things and doing annual check-ups with your advisors, you should limit surprises and be able to relax.

It's your time to enjoy retirement. You have earned it!

PART TWO: **ENJOYING YOUR RETIREMENT LIFESTYLE**

There is more to retirement considerations than just the financial impact. When you were working as a dentist, you felt needed, you served your community with valuable healthcare, and you developed many long friendships with hundreds of people. Upon retirement, all that stops. In addition, by the time retirement comes, your kids may have graduated from college and are on their own. All that clinical experience in dentistry has little use in day-to-day life now. You begin a new life and have many choices. You can learn a new set of skills (photography, art, etc.) or get some new hobbies or enjoy new activities or enjoy travelling. Without having a vision of retirement, many dentists start to cycle back into their thoughts and think about continuing to work a little longer. If you have something to look forward to after you retire, it will make the transition process more exciting. If you do continue to work, even part-time, it helps to keep you connected to the community, keeps you active, and brings in a little extra spending money.

SOME OPTIONS FOR A RETIRED DENTIST

You could go into teaching. The schools are always looking for experienced dentists to work in the clinics. You could even teach at a dental assisting or dental hygiene school. Someone with clinical experience can certainly pass down value to new students.

You could work part-time in some of the local dental charities or mobile clinics. There are plenty of opportunities and need for Dentists Without Borders for those willing to travel abroad and help with badly needed dental care.

You could go into consulting. New dentists are always looking for assistance with decisions. The dentists who make the fewest "bad" decisions tend to win the game. There are many investments and marketing scams out there that benefit the marketers more than the dentists or the patients. There are also some pieces of equipment that have "debatable" value as regards ability to generate the investment needed to make them worthwhile purchasing. These kinds of coaching ideas can not only make a dentist money but also save a dentist money.

You could spend the time with your family. Sometimes dentists can be perfectionist workaholics and they simply need to stop working and take the time to smell the roses and enjoy their families. Get some hobbies or begin an exercise program so that you can live long enough to enjoy your retirement!

You could join one of a number of Community Service Clubs. There are several organizations that are always looking for people with time on their hands to pull off community events or programs for specific groups of needy people.

Stay healthy! Your health is your wealth. Keep active, read, exercise, eat wisely and keep learning!

REFERENCES AND RESOURCES

The American Dental Education Association
www.adea.org

American Dental Association Website
www.ada.org

DentistryIQ has a wealth of articles on the business of dentistry
http://www.dentistryiq.com/

BizFilings.com has a wealth of information online about incorporating your business. http://www.bizfilings.com/

Critical Trends Affecting the Future of Dentistry – prepared for the ADA March 2013 by Diringer and Associates

The Fate of a Legendary Practice – A publication of the Muma College of Business at the University of South Florida September 22, 2016
http://pubs.mumacasereview.org/2016/MCR-01-09-Oscher-LegendaryPractice-p1-18.pdf

Wells Fargo Practice Financing for Dentists
https://practicefinance.wellsfargo.com/dentists/practice-financing-programs/

The Checklist Manifesto, author Atul Gawande
2011 BVR's GUIDE TO VALUING DENTAL PRACTICES by author Stanley Pollock, BS, DMD, MS, PhD, JD, MCBA, MCMEA, ABAR

Health, United States, 2016 With Chartbook on Long-term Trends in Health published by the U.S. Department of Health and Human Services, Centers for Disease Control and Prevention, National Center for Health Statistics
https://www.cdc.gov/nchs/data/hus/hus16.pdf

Note: Since we cannot control if these articles will be at these website URL's in the future, we have also included them on the website www.DentalBusinessStrategy. com for your convenience.

Appendix

This book is one of the several books in the Dental Business Strategy Series. Please visit our website www.DentalBusinessStrategy.com for more information about our other books as well as coaching services available. There may also be supplemental articles to help you with your business there as well.

We offer a complimentary no-obligation strategy session call for dentists who have purchased this book. You may sign up for that online at the web site above.

We recognize that the dental field is constantly changing, just as marketing and technology is changing. If you have feedback or input for future editions of this book, please email it to: support@DentalBusinessStrategy.com

The Dental Practice Strategy Guidebook was written with all stages in the dental career in mind. In addition to discussing Emerging Trends in Dentistry, this book introduces "The Dental Practice Mastery Matrix". This is a powerful tool for analyzing your business options and developing effective leadership and marketing strategies for running a Dental Practice.

This updated comprehensive guide covers all aspects of dentistry including the various Dental Practice Models such as:

- Solo Practice
- Associateships
- Partnerships
- Group Practices
- Space Sharing
- Solo Group Practices
- Corporate Dentistry

Dr. Randall LaFrom had a successful practice in Silicon Valley, California for over 34 years. He was an early integrator of many high-technologies including dental lasers, CAD/CAM porcelain crown milling, and the use of the 3D ConeBeam to assist with dental implants, oral surgery, and root canals. Throughout his career, he was an employee, he was in a space-sharing arrangement, he started a practice from scratch, he had associates, he had a solo group practice, and successfully transitioned from his practice. He has been a trainer for various dental equipment manufacturers and helped lead a Dental Study Club in Silicon Valley for over 12 years. He has spoken to study clubs and small groups, and with the effective coaching of Scott Manning, MBA, of *Dental Success Today*,

 he was able to transition into retirement and is now a mentor and coaching other dentists in their practices.

Scott Manning, MBA and Randall LaFrom, DDS

DENTAL PRACTICE STRATEGY GUIDEBOOK